TORAH FOR
MENTAL HEALTH

TORAH FOR MENTAL HEALTH

Jewish Wisdom for Psychological Growth

Rabbi Dr. Tal Sessler, PhD

Universal-Publishers
Irvine • Boca Raton

Torah for Mental Health:
Jewish Wisdom for Psychological Growth

Universal Publishers, Inc.
Irvine • Boca Raton
USA • 2025
www.Universal-Publishers.com

ISBN: 978-1-59942-753-9 (pbk.)
ISBN: 978-1-59942-754-6 (ebk.)
ISBN: 978-1-59942-755-3 (aud.)

Typeset by Medlar Publishing Solutions Pvt Ltd, India
Cover design by Ivan Popov

Library of Congress Cataloging-in-Publication Data

Names: Sessler, Tal, 1977- author.
Title: Torah for mental health : Jewish wisdom for psychological growth / Rabbi Dr. Tal Sessler, PhD.
Description: Irvine, CA : Universal Publishers, 2025. | Summary: "The world breaks everyone, and afterward many are strong at the broken places, observed Ernest Hemingway in his youth. By fixing and integrating ourselves, taught Rabbi Isaac Luria in the 16th century, we also contribute to the grand cosmic endeavor of universal healing and repair. This book offers sustained reflections about what the Torah has to say about seminal emotive states such as anxiety, fear, depression, empathy, resilience, post traumatic growth, anger and self-compassion, to name but a few. The book also explores how to attain spiritual and psychological virtues such as forgiveness, letting go of resentments, as well as the cultivation of humility, integrity, motional intelligence and active listening. If you are interested in dialogues between Torah wisdom and various contemporary and classical psychological modalities, then this book will meet your needs. If you are thirsting for a Torah which goes beyond legalistic minutiae, a Torah which is suffused in core life issues and challenges, then this book is for you"-- Provided by publisher.
Identifiers: LCCN 2025000609 (print) | LCCN 2025000610 (ebook) |
    ISBN 9781599427539 (paperback) | ISBN 9781599427546 (ebook)
Subjects: LCSH: Self-actualization (Psychology)--Biblical teaching. |
    Self-actualization (Psychology)--Religious aspects--Judaism. |
    Self-consciousness (Awareness)--Biblical teaching. | Self-consciousness (Awareness)--
    Religious aspects--Judaism. | Bible. Pentateuch--Criticism, interpretation, etc.
Classification: LCC BF637.S4 S48 2025 (print) | LCC BF637.S4 (ebook) |
    DDC 296.7--dc23/eng/20250115
LC record available at https://lccn.loc.gov/2025000609
LC ebook record available at https://lccn.loc.gov/2025000610

To T.E., who guides with wisdom and compassion.

In remembrance of Parviz Danielpour,
a gentle man of blessed memory.

With gratitude to Dr. Donna Miller
who sanctifies God's name in her work, and
who gave me a shot at a new career and calling.

Table of Contents

Brokenness: A Primordial State

"The world breaks everyone, and afterward many are strong at the broken places," observed Ernest Hemingway in his youth.

Kabbalah, the medieval Jewish mystical tradition, teaches us that divinity itself is also scattered and fragmented.

According to the Kabbalah, the world itself came into being as a result of a cosmic shattering known as "the breaking of the vessels."

By fixing and integrating ourselves, taught Rabbi Isaac Luria in the 16th century, we also contribute to the universal endeavor of cosmic healing and repair.

In psalm 147, which Jews recite daily as part of the morning service, God is described as a psychotherapist.

Specifically, God is described in psalm 147 as "the healer of shattered hearts," who also "bandages our sadnesses."

This book offers sustained reflections about what the Torah has to say about seminal emotive states such as anxiety, fear, depression, empathy, resilience, post traumatic growth, anger and self-compassion, to name but a few.

The book also explores how to attain spiritual and psychological virtues such as forgiveness, letting go of resentments, as well as the cultivation of humility, integrity, emotional intelligence and active listening.

If you are interested in dialogues between Torah wisdom and various contemporary and classical psychological modalities, then this book will meet your needs.

Above all, if you are thirsting for a Torah which goes beyond legalistic minutiae, a Torah which is suffused in core life issues and challenges, then this book is for you.

May you continue to grow in soul, and draw spiritual sustenance and emotive strength from the profound reservoirs of Jewish spiritual wisdom.

Gratitude & Mindfulness: How to Spiritually Survive Captivity

How did the two of the captives who were rescued from Gaza in 2024 spiritually survive captivity?

Noa Argamani shared that she prayed every day, and that she also engaged in mindfulness practices.

Andrei Kozlov kept a diary. A gratitude journal. Every day he wrote one line in his journal: "Today is a gift."

The ability to behold every day as a precious gift in the inferno of Hamas captivity is a monumental spiritual achievement.

At times we all feel overwhelmed by life's interminable material and psychological demands. We don't always feel grateful every day for the precious gift of life.

But Andrei Kozlov was grateful every day. Stripped of his liberty, he maintained his inner freedom.

Through mindfulness and gratitude, Noa Argamni and Andrei Kozlov maintained their sanity and inner equilibrium.

Long before they were physically liberated, they overcame their inner prisons. They constantly rekindled the light of hope and faith in their souls.

They are our heroes, and they are our teachers.

Their invincible spirit is testament to the eternity of the Jewish people, and to the miracle of Israel as "the victory of possibility over probability."

Vulnerability: A Godly Attribute

A wise Bible scholar was once asked who is the most tragic figure in the entire Hebrew Bible.

The scholar responded by saying that God is the most tragic figure in the Bible, because God expects great things from us, and we keep on breaking God's heart.

The creation of humanity was an act of supreme cosmic vulnerability on God's behalf.

According to the Kabbalah, the Infinite One withdrew some of its primordial metaphysical light, in order to make room for the creation of a physical universe.

By creating the human person in the divine image, God took a risk by imbuing the world with a reflective being who can create but also devastate and annihilate the planet.

In other words, God was being vulnerable, and God took a chance on us.

The courage to be vulnerable, to take an emotional risk by exposing to another person our innermost feelings and thoughts, is an act of supreme psychological courage.

It is also a God-like gesture.

The late Israeli statesman Shimon Peres was once asked why he trusted Prime Minister Rabin during the last years of the latter's life.

I trusted Rabin, said Shimon Peres (I'm paraphrasing), because when you trust someone you might get disappointed and even betrayed at times, but if you never get out of your shell and reach out in vulnerability to another person, you will always lose out.

Shimon Peres was right to observe that in the absence of vulnerability in our lives we will always "lose out", because without vulnerability there is no true love or connection.

Without emotional vulnerability, observed Dr. Brene Brown, we condemn ourselves to a life suffused with shame and fear, a life devoid of veritable and enduring happiness and joy.

"The unexamined life is not worth living," argued Socrates. Perhaps.

But surely a life devoid of deep connections, trust and creativity is not a life worth living either.

These core ingredients of the human condition necessitate openness and vulnerability.

It is therefore essential for us to summon the courage to be emotionally vulnerable.

Take it from God.

Resilience: Building New Worlds

In 2013, I moved to Los Angeles, in order to serve as rabbi for the Sephardic Community.

The community was varied and diverse, and included Jews who were born in different Middle-Eastern countries, such as Egypt and Iran.

Coming from an Ashkenazi-European background, and having only served Ashkenazi synagogues before that, I mistakenly thought that the Jewish-Mizrahi story is completely different than the European-Ashkenazi story.

I couldn't have been more wrong.

With time, I discovered some striking similarities between the fate and destiny of European and Middle-Eastern Jewry.

Both communities were culturally and financially thriving communities which contributed much to the non-Jewish environment.

Both communities had to traumatically rebuild their lives elsewhere, after Jewish existence was no longer tenable in their respective homelands.

And finally—and perhaps most importantly—both communities exhibited astonishing resilience, by replanting themselves in Israel and North America in the second half of the 20th century.

In arguably the most famous verse in all of scripture, the Torah starts its narrative by stating that in a beginning, God created the heaven and the earth.

In a midrash (rabbinic teaching), the sages ask what did the Almighty "do" prior to the creation of the world.

The rabbis' astounding answer is that prior to the creation of the world, the Holy Blessed One used to "create worlds, and then destroy them."

Rabbi Joseph Soloveitchik teaches us that the fact that God "persevered", and went on to rebuild new worlds after their destruction, is a teaching for us to also rebuild our own inner worlds, after they are shattered and destroyed.

We have all known the pain and anguish of loving relationships which failed to endure in the long-run.

We have also known the death of loved ones, and mourned their loss and the void that they left in our hearts.

However, teaches the Rav, we are to follow in the Almighty's ways, and rebuild our own inner worlds after calamity strikes, move on after processing and mourning, and gradually and gingerly rebuild our lives.

That is what countless Jewish communities, from east and west, achieved from time immemorial, since the very dawn and genesis of Jewish exile, and this is what we, as private individuals, are also summoned to achieve as well, in our own personal lives.

Following in the footsteps of our ancestors entails not only the preservation and enhancement of Jewish spirituality.

It is also testament to the undying resilience of the Jewish people, and the tenacious spirit of God's eternal people.

Gratitude: A Family Tradition

Every weekday morning, I am blessed to take my daughters to school.

And each time we get into the car, my daughters ask me for my phone, because they want to listen to music on my Spotify app.

I always agree to their request on one condition.

Firstly, each of them needs to first say out loud one thing that they're grateful for this morning.

After that, I give them my phone.

Once I hand my daughters my phone, I always recite my own gratitude list, thanking God for all the manifold spiritual and physical blessings in my life.

I created this daily ritual, which I am very strict and meticulous about, because we human beings are prone to "negativity bias"—a notorious human disposition to focus more on that which is lacking and not working in our lives.

In the Torah portion of Vayishlach, Jacob is about to return to Israel after having amassed a great fortune abroad, and against all odds.

Jacob left Israel as a lonely and penniless refugee.

Jacob's self-made fortune and large family constitute a precursor to Jewish prosperity and familism centuries and millennia thereafter to this very day.

Jacob remembers his humble origins. He says to the Almighty: "I am belittled by all the countless acts of loving-kindness that You have bestowed upon me, Your faithful servant. For I had nothing with me but a rod, when I first traversed the river Jordan."

Like Jacob, my paternal grandfather was also a refugee. A Holocaust refugee.

One day, hungry and cold in the ferocious Moscow winter of 1940, my grandfather asked a Soviet Jewish soldier to share his bread with him—a hungry Jewish refugee from Nazi Germany. The soldier agreed.

Because of that, I developed over the years a personal custom to meditate upon this family story whenever I recite the Jewish blessing over the bread. Because I remember who I am, and because I remember where I come from.

"Those who have the ability to be grateful, are also the ones who also have the ability to achieve greatness," observed behavioral scientist Steve Maraboli.

The Hebrew word for "Jew" יהודי, contains the exact same letters as the Hebrew word הודייה, which means "gratitude."

To be a Jew, not merely by way of mere ethnic lineage—but also by way of sheer spiritual profundity, means to master the rarified art of a life suffused with cosmic gratitude to God Almighty.

Cosmic Empathy: The God Who Cares

Hermann Cohen was a great Jewish philosopher.

Cohen's book "Religion of Reason Out of the Sources of Judaism," is a very complicated philosophical work of religious ethics.

There is a story about a pious Chassidic Jew who came to see Hermann Cohen, in order to try to understand Cohen's intricate philosophy.

When Cohen was done explaining his philosophy to the Chassid, the latter asked Cohen: "But where is the Creator of the world in all of this?"

According to the story, the philosopher responded to this pietistic probe by sobbing.

This beautiful story captures the unbridgeable theological gulf between Aristotle's God—a philosophical-conceptual God, and the Jewish experience of God as a pervasive spiritual presence permeating the cosmos and the human spirit at the same time.

The Jewish God is an engaged God, who is invested in the unfolding of the human story, the Jewish story, and our individual life-stories as well.

In Exodus 7:3 we find an exquisite exemplification of the notion of a caring God.

God says to Moses at the burning bush that He heard "the cry" of the Jewish people, and that He also knows "their pain."

The notion of an empathic God who knows our pain and hears our cries is instrumental to the Jewish story.

Like God, Moses was also a supremely empathic being.

Moses exemplified his empathy when he protected Jethro's daughters from harassment, when he compassionately took care of the sheep he shepherded, when he chose his Jewish birth family over his adopting Egyptian family, and when he protected a Hebrew slave from the cruelty of an Egyptian taskmaster.

Empathy, the human ability to be attuned to the feelings and emotive plights of other people, is a highly evolved and imperative psychological capacity.

In a place where there is empathy, redemption can begin.

And in a place where instead of empathy we find apathy—the worst atrocities known to humankind can continue to occur unnoticed.

For as Elie Wiesel did well to observe: "The opposite of love is not hate. The opposite of love is indifference."

Letting Go of the Past

In the Torah portion of Vayera, Lot's wife looks back at the ruinous cities of Sodom and Gomorrah and perishes.

This is a very enigmatic scene. Why did Lot's wife perish and turn into a pillar of salt on account of gazing at the devastation?

One way to understand this cryptic story is on a psychologically symbolic level. The idea of being transfixed and utterly obsessed by yesteryear's tragedies and traumas is at work here.

Some people become so shackled to their tragic past to the extent that they exclusively keep on "looking back" reactively, and fail to move forward proactively.

Such people are prisoners of their past. They develop a victim mentality, and fail to move ahead.

Sometimes entire nations can drown themselves in self-pity, and fail to move forward and face the future.

On the other hand, there are also forward-looking nations who cherish and remember the past, but ultimately they live in the present and are future-oriented.

The Jewish story in the last eight decades is a clear case in point.

During the second half of the 20th century, about a million Jews had to leave their homes and possessions in Islamic countries. Many of them were forcibly displaced and expelled.

Countries like Iran, Iraq, Yemen, Libya, Lebanon, Syria, Algeria, Egypt, Tunisia and Morocco used to house many hundreds of thousands of Jews for thousands of years.

Overwhelmingly, most of these hundreds of thousands of Jewish refugees from Islamic lands had to leave their indigenous homes and possessions behind, and to rebuild their lives anew from nothing and with nothing, in other lands in Europe, North America, and Israel.

Unlike Lot's wife, the Jewish refugees from Islamic lands were not transfixed by the past.

They moved forward. They educated their children, they acquired professions, they built a future. They were resilient and proactive.

The same applies to Holocaust refugees and survivors like my grandfather and his brother.

My grandfather and his brother were the sole survivors from a large family. They never felt sorry for themselves or drowned in self-pity.

I never heard my grandfather say that the Germans are responsible for his current life conditions and existential predicament.

My grandfather and his brother were too busy building and sowing. They simply didn't make the time to be drowned by the agonies and the injustice of the past. They were too busy being forward-looking people.

They remembered and commemorated the past, they honored the deceased, they carried within them the emotional scars and the irredeemable pain, but they were not held hostage by the past.

To be a Jew is to offer humanity a sustained tutorial in self-overcoming and existential resilience.

Let us learn from our mentors in life, our parents and grandparents, who rebuilt their lives with tenacity and inner strength.

Let us walk in their light, and emulate their ways.

Affirming Life: When Moses Overcame a Breakdown

What do Martin Luther King, Abraham Lincoln, Golda Meir and Leo Tolstoy all have in common?

They all contemplated suicide at one point in their lives.

In a stunning biblical passage (Numbers 11:15), Moses also conveys to God that if the current state of affairs persists, then he too, would rather die than continue living.

In the "Myth of Sisyphus," authored by French novelist and essayist Albert Camus, the question of suicide is a recurrent leitmotif.

Camus, a staunch atheist, grappled with the problem of atheistic meaninglessness, and why should one continue living in a world devoid of a godly presence.

Conversely, Friedrich Nietzsche, the most brilliant atheistic philosopher of modern European thought, observed that "He who has a why to live, can bear almost any how."

By this the philosopher meant to say that when we have a profound underlying spiritual reason to live, we will persevere and overcome seemingly insurmountable obstacles.

Nietzsche's view was corroborated by the findings and observations made by psychiatrist Dr. Viktor Frankl, after his time in Auschwitz.

Frankl, who founded the psychological approach of logotherapy, postulated that we humans are the "meaning seeking animal," and that indeed, when we have a resounding reason to live, we can overcome great adversity.

Golda Meir and Winston Churchill overcame their depressions, and found purpose in saving their countries from the menace of perdition.

Tolstoy and Martin Luther King, like Moses, reaffirmed life by reinvigorating their faith in God, and by leading a life of saintly dedication to the common good.

Professor Martin Seligman, founder of Positive Psychology, teaches us that we find meaning when we harness our strengths and virtues "in the service of something larger" than our solitary individual selves.

"Behold I have given before you life and death, and a blessing and a curse, and you shall choose life, so that you and your descendants shall live," said Moses after having overcome his own personal breakdown (Deuteronomy 30:19).

We choose life because of love, because of faith and higher strivings, and because of the intrinsic sanctity of life itself.

Dancing Freedom: Exiting Our Inner Prisons

At the young age of 95, Dr. Edith Eger published her second book.

In this book, entitled "The Gift," Dr. Eger, who survived the inferno of Auschwitz, argues that the mental and emotional inner prisons that we build around ourselves are even more restrictive than physical prisons.

According to Dr. Eger, the foundation of human freedom lies in our ability to make choices in life, and embark upon a psychological exodus from confining inner prisons such as victimhood, shame, rigidity and fear.

Befittingly, Dr. Eger calls her therapeutic approach "Choice Therapy."

In one of the most mystical passages in the entire Torah, Moses asks God to convey and articulate the divine essence.

God's cryptic and laconic answer to Moses' audacious request is three words in the Hebrew, which in English mean: "I Will Be What I Will Be."

In other words, God is infinite and spiritual, and thus also beyond human articulation, definition, categorization or thematization.

Notice that God's answer to Moses ("I Will Be What I Will Be") is rendered in the future tense.

God's essence is thus future-oriented and open-ended.

Similarly, since we are all fashioned in the divine image, ours is also a future-oriented and open-ended destiny.

In other words, we are radically free.

Dr. Eger's clinical approach of "Choice Therapy," is thus deeply entrenched in Jewish spiritual consciousness.

Much of our human dignity stems from the fact that even in the direst of circumstances, our fate might be physically sealed, but our spirit can always be free.

In her riveting book, Dr. Eger recounts how she was forced to dance before a satanic senior Nazi officer during her time in Auschwitz, at the tender age of 16, after both her parents were gassed to death.

Eger writes that as she was dancing before the angel of death, she internally observed the Nazi's irredeemable evil essence, and how she, stripped of any material possessions, is more spiritually and morally liberated then he is.

If Edith Eger felt free whilst literally dancing before the angel of death, we can also dance our way through life, despite life's manifold trials and tribulations.

Let us dance in her light, and emulate her way.

Wounded Healer: Joseph's Spiritual Metamorphosis

Young Jospeh was a self-absorbed and arrogant youth.

Joseph dreamed of actualizing his manifold talents and gifts, in order to achieve social approbation and familial admiration.

However, Joseph's haughtiness instigated the enmity of his siblings, and even the reproach of his loving father.

With time, Joseph was humbled by life. The cruelty of his brothers, his years of servitude and wrongful imprisonment, all these gave rise to a spiritual lowliness of ego.

Later on, Joseph's meteoric rise to economic power made him overnight the world's chief nutritional provider.

Joseph literally nourished the entire ancient Near East.

According to the Chassidic tradition, Joseph was also a spiritual provider, and his Torah sustained his family in Egypt.

Exhibiting astonishing selflessness, Joseph cleansed himself of any shred of resentment and malice towards his brothers who sold him into slavery, and came to see everything that happened to him as divinely orchestrated by the hand of providence.

Joseph, who suffered much in his youth, ultimately became a wounded healer.

A wounded healer, according to Carl Jung, is someone who feels compelled to help others because he himself is "wounded"—namely grappling with some internal psychic injury.

British psychotherapist Alison Barr found in her research that approximately 74% of mental health practitioners had experienced some emotive injuries which ultimately led them to pursue their career of choice.

In another study, this time conducted in the US and Canada by Victor et al. (2021), the findings demonstrated that no less than 82% of current psychology graduate students and faculty had experienced some inner wound which led them to pursue their career of choice.

In his work "The Silence of Heaven," Israeli novelist and essayist Amos Oz argues that every great writer writes "from an inner wound," and that "the deeper the wound, the greater the writing."

Joseph's astonishing spiritual metamorphosis from cosmic narcissism (the dream of being worshipped by the sun and the moon) to ultimate altruism (providing spiritual and physical nourishment to all), is an inspiring story about the human capacity to achieve greatness by way of post traumatic growth.

It should serve all of us as a sustained tutorial in terms of how to convert suffering into service, pain into benevolence, and hopelessness to helpfulness.

Anxiety & Politics: Overcoming Fear

I was fourteen years old when I first experienced political terror. It was during the first Gulf War, and I was taking shelter with my family in Tel Aviv from the menace of Iraqi Scud missiles.

I remember my ten year old brother shaking like a leaf as the windows of the apartment were trembling on account of the missiles exploding only three miles away from our home.

I also knew geo-political terror in high school, as buses were being blown up by suicide bombers in Tel Aviv, and we were barred from exiting the school premises during recess. It wasn't safe.

When I was 23 years old, I saw the smoke arising from the Twin Towers from the street corner of my Upper East Side apartment in Manhattan.

It was September 11th 2001, and once again I was only a handful of miles away, this time from the deadliest terror attack in history.

Living with political uncertainty and inner terror, whether in Europe or the Middle East, has been a hallmark feature of the Jewish exilic condition for countless centuries.

In the prophetic reading (haftarah) adjacent to the Torah portion of Bo, the prophet Jeremiah also acts as a geo-political commentator.

Jeremiah prophesies the descent of ancient Egypt as a regional hegemonic superpower, and the rise of Babylonia as a newly emerging dominant power in ancient Near-Eastern geo-politics.

In this context, Jeremiah beseeches the people to "have no fear" twice, and in two separate and successive verses (Jeremiah 46:27-28).

In war-torn regions, mental health practitioners indeed endeavor, like Jeremiah did, to decrease the levels of inner terror and political anxiety which stem from the emotional aftershocks of armed conflict.

In Israel specifically, there is a highly voluminous psychological literature pertaining to inter-generational transmission of trauma, as many Israeli citizens are descendants of refugees and survivors.

"I shall speak and find comfort," states the book of Job (Job 32:20).

This ancient biblical intuition, that we can find catharsis and healing in articulating our traumas and pain, became salient in a post-Freudian world.

In "Anxiety and Politics," German-Jewish theorist Franz Neumann employed Freudian political psychology in an effort to better understand blind political obedience.

In the immortal words of Thomas Paine, we live in "times that try men's souls."

Those of us who recognize our common humanity as individuals created in the divine image must labor hard to build bridges across political schisms, whether within our extended families, communities, social circles, or humanity at large—as far as all peace-loving people are concerned.

But in order to achieve all that, we must first and foremost attend to our own personal and collective traumas and inner wounds.

We can begin, in the timeless words of Rabbi Nachman of Breslov, by recalling that even in an age infested with global terror, our world is still akin to "a very narrow bridge," and that the most important thing to recall, is that we do not have to become permanently shackled and emotionally immobilized by political anxiety and inner fears.

After all, it was President FDR who had a distinctly Chassidic moment, when he observed during a critical historical juncture fraught with political anxiety and inner terror that "the only thing we have to fear is fear itself."

Self-Compassion & Radical Acceptance: When Moses Forgave Himself

A couple of months ago, I met a woman who was in profound agony.

The woman shared with me that she is haunted and held emotionally captive by a decision which she made more than two years ago.

The woman told me that a couple of years ago, she had severe doubts about the long-term viability of her marriage, and decided to move out of the apartment in which she lived with her husband.

Several months later, this woman had a change of heart, and decided that she would like to reconcile with her husband, from whom she was separated at this stage.

But it was too late. Apparently, the woman's husband felt that he could no longer trust his wife's commitment to their marriage, and filed for divorce.

Despite all the woman's pleas and supplications, her husband remained steadfast and resolute in his decision to terminate the marriage.

As time passed, the woman grew more and more desperate and emotionally devastated.

Two years later, despite the passage of time, she is still stuck in an intense mourning cycle, and blames herself for the failure of her marriage.

For over two years now, this woman hasn't been able to practice "radical acceptance," and to come to grips with the fact that her marriage is over.

Since she was the one who first initiated the separation and moved out of the family home, this woman is having a very hard time with practicing self-compassion and self-forgiveness.

In the book of Deuteronomy, Moses prays fervently, and begs God to rescind the heavenly decree according to which he, Moses, will not be allowed to enter the promised land with the rest of the people of Israel.

Moses did not fulfill in a satisfactory way a divine instruction, and the severe punishment was for him to die in the desert.

Despite Moses' interminable spiritual pleadings, the heavenly decree was not averted, and Moses was barred from realizing his life-long dream of setting foot in the promised land.

"No person leaves this world with even half of their wishes fulfilled," states the rabbinic midrash in Kohelet Rabbah.

Most of our wants and cravings will simply not come into fruition and be realized in our lifetime.

Furthermore, sometimes our demise might even inadvertently be of our own doing, like the woman who initiated the separation from her husband, and like Moses' failure to adhere to the divine decree.

Practicing radical acceptance when we cannot change a given situation or reverse the clock, is a very powerful psychological tool, which prevents our pain from turning into excruciating suffering.

Radical acceptance enables us to move on with our lives and to also practice self-compassion, to forgive ourselves for past mistakes.

Reinhold Niebuhr, a 20th century American theologian, coined the Serenity Prayer, which reads as follows:

"God, grant me the serenity to accept the things I cannot change, the courage to change the things I can, and the wisdom to know the difference."

May we learn, like Moses, to ultimately accept that which is sealed and cannot be changed, and to summon the resolve to proactively change that which we can still effect.

Anti-Fragility: Raising Stronger Children

When I was ten years old, my family and I moved from Tel Aviv to London.

My English wasn't up to par, and I spent my first year in London working on improving my proficiency and command of the English language.

Once I turned eleven years old, I felt more comfortable in London, and my parents actually encouraged me to take the bus alone to school.

Today, for many parents, the idea of letting their kid take the bus alone in a foreign city and a large urban metropolis is quite unthinkable.

Social psychologist Jonathan Haidt thinks that this is a mistake.

According to Professor Haidt, we over protect our children today, and thereby make them actually weaker—more fragile and sensitive to conflict and adversity.

This is related to the concept of "Anti-Fragility," which was developed by professor Nassim Taleb of New York University.

Anti-Fragility is about getting stronger through adversity and hardship.

Anti-fragility is not the same as resilience. Resilience is about preserving my original state despite external pressure. Anti-fragility is bigger than that.

Anti-Fragility is about actually becoming stronger than I was before.

The immune system is an example of anti-fragility. The immune system actually needs to be exposed to certain viruses in order to become more resistant.

Jewish history is a sustained tutorial in anti-fragility.

In the opening chapter of the book of Exodus, the dehumanization and persecution of the Jews of Egypt is described in detail.

However, the Torah also stresses that the ancient Israelites had a very peculiar and unique quality: "The more they were tortured, the more they grew in tenacity and strength" (Exodus 1:12).

If we want our descendants to be anti-fragile, then we need to learn how to step back sometimes and let them stumble and fall occasionally, as they endeavor to find their footing independently in a demanding and stressful world.

Teach your children to deal with conflict and adversity. Don't switch classes or schools just because of a strict teacher or a challenging fellow student.

Once our children grow up, they might actually encounter an overly demanding boss or a ruthless colleague.

Help your descendants prepare for life in the real world by cultivating anti-fragility in them, the same way that our ancestors have been mentoring humanity in the fine art of anti-fragility from time immemorial.

Cosmic Sadness: When God was Grief-Stricken

It is said that a towering scholar once asked a great rabbi to ponder who is the most tragic character in the entire Hebrew Bible.

The rabbi conjectured that the most tragic character in the Bible might be Moses or King Saul.

No, exclaimed the scholar, the most tragic figure in the entire Bible is God Almighty Himself, because God expects great things from us, individually and collectively, and yet we keep on shattering God's heart.

This exquisite anecdote finds credence in the opening Torah portion, in which God becomes "saddened to His core" (Genesis 6:6), after having observed the pervasive evil streak inherent in the human condition.

Strikingly, God is the only figure in the entire Bible who is depicted as "saddened." The Hebrew root for "sadness," (עצב) does not describe any other biblical figure.

It was Immanuel Kant who did well to describe humanity as a "crooked timber," as a warped piece of wood that cannot be rendered completely symmetrical and straight.

That being said, even though humanity might well be incorrigible, the world as a whole is still redeemable, insists Jewish theology.

Exhibiting relentless hopefulness and optimism, Jewish theology believes in the prospect of dialectical redemption for humankind.

Three times a day, every weekday, Jews steadfastly pray for קרן ישועה, for forthcoming particular and universal redemption.

Sadness is a hallmark feature of the human condition. No life is bereft of times of crisis and heartache, and almost moments of despair.

Depression, argues psychologist Tal Ben Shahar, is a state of sadness devoid of hope.

Hope, insists Rabbi Jonathan Sacks, is an active virtue, in which we strive to ameliorate the individual and collective state of affairs by exerting effort and proactivity.

In his seminal work "Authentic Happiness," founder of positive psychology Martin Seligman demonstrates with empirical data that optimistic people are healthier and more successful than pessimistic people, and that optimism is a dynamic and acquired trait that can be achieved through rigorous mental and intellectual exercise.

Life is suffering, postulates the Buddhist doctrine.

Judaism accepts suffering and sadness as integral and unavoidable components of the human condition, but also insists that sadness and suffering are hardly the most dominant or central facets of the human experience.

In the Bible, God overcomes His sadness, and ventures forth to establish a perpetual spiritual bond, a covenant, with humanity in its entirety, despite our incorrigible failings.

And if God has faith in us, surely we can also have faith in ourselves.

Surely we too can overcome our own griefs and sadnesses, by giving ourselves the "permission to be human," by accepting the inevitability of periods of sadness, by proactively articulating and confronting sadness, and by leaning on other people while striving to transition from "a eulogy into a dance" (Psalm 30).

Forgiveness: Letting Go of Resentment

Leviticus 19:18 is one of the most famous verses in all of scripture.

Famously, in this verse God instructs us to love our fellow persons as we love ourselves.

Modern thinkers such as Freud and Nietzsche saw this commandment as inherently flawed, dangerous, or outright naive.

The Talmud brings forth a more tenable model of personal benevolence by teaching us that we should not do unto others that which is hateful unto us.

But whichever way people choose to interpret and understand the divine instruction to love other humans as we love ourselves, almost everyone tends to forget and marginalize the first and opening part of this verse (Leviticus 19:18).

Right before the Torah commands us to love others as we love ourselves, the Torah stipulates, in the very same verse, that we should desist from taking revenge or harboring resentments towards other people.

When Jews recite the nocturnal Shema prayer before falling asleep, they recite a paragraph in which they express forgiveness for anyone who may have hurt them, whether intentionally or unintentionally, whether in a material or in a psychological fashion.

Letting go of resentments and enmities is indeed imperative for sound sleep and a rage-free existence.

When we harbor resentments, we infuse our souls with emotional toxicity and mental anguish.

Rabbi Sacks once recounted how as a young and poor college student he used to carry heavy suitcases all the way from the train station to his college room.

It was an exhausting and frustrating ordeal for the rabbi to carry such a heavy and almost insurmountable burdensome weight.

Forgiveness, teaches us Rabbi Sacks, is akin to letting go of the suitcases.

Cleansing our souls of resentful malice is also part and parcel of the 12-Step process which individuals struggling with addictions undergo.

Anyone who harbors strong resentments towards other people is walking about life being held emotionally hostage and mentally captive by other people and their past misdeeds.

Letting go of hate and resentment is thus not only a majestic prelude to loving others as one loves oneself, it is also a critical and indispensable signpost on the road to mental health and emotional robustness.

Reframing: Telling Yourself a Different Story

Rachel Edri is a national hero in Israel.

On October Seventh, five terrorists entered Rachel's house, and took her and her husband David hostage.

In a TV interview, Rachel told the journalists how she saved her own life.

Rachel said that she decided to look at her dire situation from a completely different angle, and to think about the terrorists holding a grenade above her head simply as house guests who need to be hosted and entertained.

Instead of panicking and begging for her life, Rachel "became friends" with the terrorists.

She served them food and made them coffee and chatted with them.

Eventually, miraculously, when Rachel and her husband were rescued by Israeli special forces, the terrorists didn't shoot Rachel, probably because they humanized Rachel after she chatted with them, hosted them, and was warm and gracious towards them.

In many ways, what saved Rachel's life was her decision to reframe the story of her own situation while being kidnapped by terrorists.

Telling herself a different story, one in which she is simply hosting guests from another culture, enabled Rachel to calm down, regroup, and take control of a helpless situation.

Much of our life depends on the stories we tell ourselves about our given situation in life.

The stories we tell ourselves about what happens to us in life are called "narratives".

If we simply change the narrative of a given situation, our entire outlook and emotional situation may well change for the better.

As Jews, we always knew how to change a dire situation and reframe it by telling ourselves a different story about it.

In medieval times, Jews were often dehumanized by hosting nations, and suffered countless expulsions and massacres.

But we never internalized the heinous perspective of our murderers and oppressors.

As Jews, we kept on telling ourselves a sublime and dignified story according to which we have been chosen by God Almighty to spread truth and justice throughout the world.

Reframing our geo-political situation as a persecuted minority saved us from self-hatred and from internalizing the dehumanizing gaze of our oppressors and persecutors.

Reframing your situation in life is a vital psychological skill, and it can transform the entire quality of your inner life, emotionally and mentally.

Try and be a creative novelist of your own life circumstances, and train yourself to look positively and creatively at a challenging situation in your life, be it financially, relationally, or physically.

The very quality of our inner life often-times depends on the stories we tell ourselves about what is happening to us.

Darkness Visible: Radical Evil & Depression

Winston Churchill was a gifted painter and a towering statesman.

He was also a gifted painter in words, and coined the term "iron curtain" to describe Cold War Europe.

Churchill, who led the war against radical evil and the Nazis, also fought another mighty battle in his life.

This other battle was not a geo-political battle fought on the war front, but rather an internal battle waged internally in the trenches of the heart.

Churchill struggled throughout his life with sporadic depression, which he called his "black dog."

The first war that the Children of Israel fought as a people was waged against a pernicious enemy known historically as "Amalek."

Amalek was a group of people who attacked the people of Israel unprovoked and from the rear, mercilessly targeting the weak and the vulnerable, while the nation itself was utterly "exhausted and tired" (Deuteronomy 25:18).

The group of Amalek thus came to be known in Jewish historical consciousness as akin to prototypical Nazis, as the kind of enemy who wants to deprive you of your very physical existence ideologically, absent any territorial or material disputations.

For Rabbi Yitzchak Levi of Bardichev, a towering Chassidic sage, Amalek symbolizes not only a ferocious geo-political enemy, but also an internal foe.

Like Churchill with his dual personal battles of the political and the psychological, the Jewish mystical tradition also implies that we really wage two chief wars in our lives.

One war is a collective war, in which we historically fight against extremist groups which, in the words of Emmanuel Levinas, seek to challenge "the very humanity of man."

The second war which we wage is an emotive and mental war waged internally.

On both these fronts, we need to collaborate communally and collectively, and to empower one another with solidarity and care, if we are to emerge triumphant on both fronts.

Mid-Life Crisis: When Jacob Fought Himself

Carl Jung was a profound diagnostician of the human condition.

According to Jung, we have both an ego and a Self.

The ego, according to Jung, is about the way we adjust to reality and societal demands and expectations.

The ego is about obtaining an identity.

The Self, professes Jung, is about the cultivation of higher strivings and the desire to achieve greater spiritual self-refinement.

In the Torah, Jacob spent many decades crafting his ego by finding his personal footing in the world.

Jacob focused for many years on achieving material success and building a family.

Finally, as Jacob readies himself to return to Israel with his family and the wealth he accumulated, Jacob undergoes a nocturnal battle with an enigmatic figure in the dead of night.

According to the Torah, Jacob was "left alone, and a man struggled with him until the rising of dawn" (Genesis 32:25).

This verse begs a question: if Jacob was left all alone, who was the man who struggled with him?

One way to resolve this textual ambiguity is to suggest that Jacob was actually struggling with himself, confronting his own inner demons, and standing on the threshold of a breakthrough in terms of his own Self evolution.

In other words, Jacob underwent a mid-life crisis, during which he struggled to unify the inherent tension between the opposing traits and inclinations in his own soul.

Jacob struggled to reconcile his spiritual self with his material self, and his desire for contemplative solitude with the demands of family life.

Later on, the Torah also states that Jacob arrived in Israel as an "Ish Shalem," as a wholesome and integrated human being (Genesis 33:18).

The philosopher Hegel argued that times of peace are empty pages in the history books.

In other words, it is conflict, whether external or internal, which ultimately gives rise to novel developments in the lives of nations and individuals alike.

In his book "The Second Mountain," author David Brooks makes a very similar argument.

According to Brooks, many of us spend the first half of our lives laboring hard to build the material and emotional infrastructure of our lives. We focus on work and family.

As our kids grow older and our careers quiet down, we have an opportunity to metaphysically climb "a second mountain."

This mountain is not the mountain of worldly self-actualization, but the mountain of being externally focused on making a lasting contribution to society writ large.

As we grow older into middle age and beyond, we have the opportunity to make a spiritual commitment to being less self-focused and more "other-focused."

Rabbi Sacks called this transition the move from the "I" of authenticity, to the "We" of the common good.

At the end of the day, we will be remembered for the imprint we left on other people's souls, and not for our credentials and worldly material achievements.

Jacob understood just that. And that's why Jacob struggled with himself "until the rising of dawn," until a moment of pristine existential lucidity.

Jacob struggled with himself, in order to ultimately discern that we grow in order to give, and that we accumulate in order to also bestow upon others and share.

Diversity: Why God Loves Multiple Perspectives

In an amusing tale, a couple comes to see their rabbi for marital advice.

The wife starts off by outlining her grievances with her husband. The rabbi listens intently, and then says to her "you are right!"

Discouraged, the husband then defends himself in a sweeping monologue, after which the rabbi says: "you are right!"

After the couple leaves, the rabbi's spouse, who was eavesdropping, asks the rabbi "how can they both be right?"

The rabbi then promptly responds to his spouse by saying: "You are also right!"

Beyond the amusing anecdote, this joke captures the subtle truth that relationships are imbued with multiple perspectives.

Each one of us has a story, a plot, a narrative, which is the inner lens through which we filter and interpret life events.

The task of an emotionally evolved person is to discern that more often than not, the person with whom you are conversing also has a valid, indeed at times even complementary perspective.

God loves multiple perspectives.

In the biblical story of the Tower of Babel, the text states that back then, when the ancient skyscraper was built, the whole world comprised of only "one language and a several words" (Genesis 11:1).

Therefore, for the Natziv, a 19th century biblical commentator, the destruction of the Tower of Babel by God was not an act of punishment for human hubris, but rather— the destruction of the Tower of Babel was an act of loving-kindness, designed to spread cultural and spiritual diversity around the world.

Just like evolved people see cultural and spiritual diversity as a source for celebration rather than lamentation in the world, similarly—we would also do well to recognize that deeply ingrained in the grand cosmic scheme of things is the notion that we carry different but equally valid emotional prisms through which we inhabit the world and experience reality.

The ability to hold multiple perspectives that different people have for the same event is a hallmark feature of successful and enduring relationships.

May we cultivate this precious outlook, for the very fate of our most cherished relationships hinges upon it.

Individuation: Realizing Your Spiritual Potential

In 1972, several months before he died, Abraham Joshua Heschel gave an extensive TV interview.

In this interview, Heschel said that the meaning of life is "to build a life as if it were a work of art."

Nietzsche beseeched us to "live dangerously," whereas Heschel implored us to live creatively.

The greatest figures in the Torah were spiritually "self-made."

Abraham and Moses gradually grew into piety and engagement, they weren't necessarily born into greatness.

In the words of Shakespeare: "Some are born great, some achieve greatness, and some have greatness thrust upon them."

Abraham and Moses achieved greatness in their own merit. Abraham and Moses both grew up in an idolatrous household.

According to the midrash, Abraham's father sold and worshipped statues, whereas Moses grew up in the home of a man who worshipped himself.

Both Abraham and Moses were old men by the time they reached their full spiritual maturation and potential.

Abraham was 75 years old when he commenced his spiritual journey, and Moses was 80 years old when he first experienced divine revelation.

Freud believed that the gist of our personality is fashioned and determined in our early years.

The Torah, like Carl Jung—the founder of analytic psychology, argues that we reach the full integration and cohesion of our personality well into the fifth decade of our lives and beyond.

Jung called this dynamic and life-long process of self-actualization "individuation."

Jethro, Moses' brother in law, is a clear case of advanced age individuation.

Jethro was a grandfather by the time he became a monotheist.

However, Jethro reached such an evolved spiritual level, that his advice to Moses determined the judicial structure of the ancient Israelites, and the Torah portion about the giving of the Ten Commandments is named after him.

This is what Heschel had in mind when he urged us to live our life "as if it were a work of art."

In an age spiritually crippled by rigid determinism and nihilistic defeatism, the Torah demonstrates that personal growth is a timeless and ageless endeavor, and that we can continue to grow in soul and positively impact the world until our dying day.

Social Oxygen: Loneliness & Human Existence

The longest study ever conducted about human happiness took place at Harvard University, and it lasted inter-generationally for over eight decades.

The title of the book based on this study is "The Good Life: Lessons from the World's Longest Scientific Study of Happiness," authored by Dr. Robert Waldinger and Dr. Marc Schulz.

According to this study, the chief indicator of overall life satisfaction and inner contentment is relationships.

The book's findings basically convey that "the stronger our relationships, the more likely we are to live happy, satisfying, and healthier lives."

People who have more robust familial, social and communal bonds are thus better poised to feel content and satisfied with their lot in life.

We all recall the collective trauma of isolation during the Covid pandemic, and how awful and emotionally painful it was to live in isolation, deprived of what I like to call "social oxygen."

In the Hebrew calendar, we celebrate the holiday of Tu Bishvat during the winter season.

In the Mishnah, according to the rabbinic school of Hillel, Tu Bishvat constitutes the new year for the trees, and is celebrated on the 15th day of the month of Shevat.

In his book "Hayey Olam" ("Eternal Life"), Rabbi Adin Steinsaltz draws an interesting parallel between the critical prerequisites for the existence of tress and humans alike.

With photosynthesis, oxygen is produced in a biological process in which light energy is converted into chemical energy.

Without oxygenic photosynthesis, most organisms in our world would simply wither away and die.

Similarly, empirical research suggests a staggering correlation between social oxygen and physical existence.

According to US Surgeon General Vivek Murthy, loneliness poses health risks as deadly as smoking about a pack of cigarettes a day.

The loneliness epidemic in our country shortens lives.

With more and more Americans opting out of membership in religious communities and organized religion, more people feel isolated and deprived of social oxygen.

The elderly are especially vulnerable.

During the High Holy Days, we stand before the Almighty and beg God: "Cast us not away in old age, as our strength leaves us, do not abandon us."

If we want God not to forsake us, it is incumbent upon us not to abandon and drop the ball on the socially vulnerable in our communities.

Invite socially vulnerable individuals to join you in attending communal and social events, reach out to them, pick up the phone to ask them how they are doing, and even consider visiting them, or inviting them over.

After all, like trees, we are all in desperate need of life-giving oxygen.

Sacred Attunement: The Virtues of Active Listening

In March 1997, King Hussein of Jordan abruptly cut short his royal visit to Spain.

The reason for the sudden change in the king's schedule was a terrible calamity in which a Jordanian soldier opened fire on Israeli school children, and murdered seven of them.

King Hussein spontaneously came to Israel, visited the homes of the deceased children, and kneeled down before the bereaved parents.

It was a sight to behold. One of the world's most celebrated and revered charismatic monarchs humbled himself in body and soul, and was utterly transfixed and attuned to the grief of the families.

The king spoke movingly and empathically, but even more than that, the king listened with intent and focus. The king was completely absorbed by the words of the bereaved.

According to humanistic psychologist Carl Rogers, active listening is key to the therapeutic process. But it goes much deeper than that.

Active listening saves marriages, and makes for good and healthy parent-child relationships.

Active listening makes for self-confident children who feel securely attached, seen and loved by their parents.

When we put down our smart phones and actually listen to each other's words and body language, we show that we care and matter to each other.

Active listening undoes the crude human inclination to hear in order to efficaciously respond, and fosters a culture of attuning ourselves to the mental and emotional universe of another person.

"It is the disease of not listening," which troubles most a character in Shakespeare's "Henry IV."

In the Book of Exodus, Moses recounts to the Israelites that redemption is imminent, and that soon they will be released from the shackles of enslavement.

Sadly, the Hebrews do not listen to Moses' prophetic words, for they are: "Out of breath, and over-worked."

How many times do we miss out on each other's words because we are "over-worked," and overtaken by other affairs in our stream of consciousness?

Listening both explicitly and implicitly is also key to economic well-being, remind us Robin Abrahams and Boris Groysberg, in "The Harvard Business Review."

If we are solely and exclusively concerned by our own emotional and mental habitat, then like the ancient Hebrews, we are enslaved to our own wants and needs, and fail to heed another person's plight or a higher calling.

To be free also entails opening up to different psychological horizons, and holding multiple perspectives in the challenging realm of inter-personal relationships.

The Gift of Choice: Freedom and Authenticity

Dr. Bernd Wollschlaeger is an unlikely Zionist and IDF officer.

His father was an ardent Nazi, and yet he chose to convert to Judaism and move to Israel.

Dr. Wollschlaeger's inspirational memoir is entitled: "A German Life: Again All Odds, Change is Possible."

In the Torah, we find a similar story about an Egyptian person who saved a Hebrew baby from the monstrous claws of genocide, despite having been the daughter of the man who swore to eradicate the Jewish people.

The rabbis named her "Bat-Ya"—which means "God's daughter," but in actuality she was pharaoh's daughter.

The stories of pharaoh's daughter and Bernd Wollschlaeger remind us that we don't have to be a passive reflection of our parental values and lifestyles.

In a world in which some serious thinkers believe in scientific determinism, Judaism remains steadfast in its belief that part of our human dignity stems from the fact that we are the autonomous authors of our own life-story. That we can break free from the confining shackles of our socialization, and become free agents.

In the 20th century, existentialist philosophers such as Heidegger, Sartre and Camus, spoke of existential "authenticity"—by which they meant living earnestly and truthfully according to your own set of values and beliefs, irrespective of any external dictates or expectations.

For the existentialists, the antithesis of "authenticity" is "bad faith" ("mauvaise foi" in French).

Bad faith is exercised when I pretend that I don't have any choices in life, that I don't have the freedom and the ability to act independently and carve out authentically my own path in life.

I remember back in the 20th century attending a book talk by a British novelist. I was a college student at the time, and not a published author yet.

The writer asked me what I would like to do with my life. I said that I would like to write books. "Listen to me," she responded, "nobody is stopping you. Nobody is stopping you."

Whether you are contemplating a change in your personal or professional life, nobody is stopping you. The choice is yours, and your life is yours to navigate and determine.

Posthumous Blessings: The Gift of Legacy

Rabbi Jonathan Sacks used to say that we live in a society with "a maximum amount of choice, and a minimum amount of meaning."

By this the rabbi meant to say that the global market economy affords us countless goods for purchase, but with hardly any underlying existential values by which to lead a life of purpose.

Furthermore, continued Rabbi Sacks, people spend months planning a party or a vacation, "but not a single day to plan a lifetime."

The idea of writing an ethical will, by which we prescribe a spiritual and moral legacy for our descendants to strive for and emulate, has deep and long roots in Jewish spirituality.

From medieval times we have the epistle of Nachmanides, in which the latter Spanish mystical sage outlines a vision for a lifetime of humility and piety for his son.

Ethical wills go all the way back to the very dawn and genesis of Jewish spiritual consciousness.

In the concluding Torah portion of the book of Genesis, Jacob bestows blessings upon his children. Each benediction is carefully crafted and delineates what are the specific strengths and deficiencies of each child.

In the prophetic literature, we also find King David prescribing to his son and future king Solomon a spiritual roadmap for a life of Torah and integrity.

In his seminal work "The Seven Habits of Highly Effective People," Stephen Covey stresses prioritizing our life vision for ourselves, and then writing a personal mission statement to ourselves, in which we are to outline the kind of people we want to be on a familial, social, professional and communal level.

Author David Brooks distinguishes in his book "The Road to Character" between "resume virtues"—our worldly external achievements, and "eulogy virtues"—the character strengths and virtues which we personified and exemplified in our lifetime.

At the end of the day, our legacy will be determined by the values we espoused and whether we managed to lead a life in which our values were in alignment with our actions.

After we die, we will not be remembered for the stuff we accumulated, but for the relationships we forged, and for that which we bestowed upon others.

To Be a Blessing: The Gift of Altruism

Abraham is the founder of monotheism.

The first commandment which Abraham receives from God is to leave his native milieu, and to inaugurate a novel spiritual and moral path for humanity elsewhere.

The second commandment that Abraham receives from on High is not about a geographical relocation, but rather—it is about a basic human orientation in life.

Abraham is commanded by God to "be a blessing" to other people, and to other nations.

Happiness, observed Kierkegaard, is "a door which opens outward."

People who lead externally focused lives derive greater inner satiation and an enduring sense of personal satisfaction.

Such people quench the human thirst to transcend the confinements of their own selfhood, by reaching out to other people with love, with compassion, with forgiveness, and with true humility and generosity of heart.

There is no vacuum in the human soul.

The soul needs to be filled by something.

The soul could be misguidedly filled by the accumulation of material assets, but that leaves you still hungry for more.

For as King Solomon observed: "A lover of money shall never be satiated with money".

The soul could also be filled by compulsive consumption of stuff and substances, and yet the inner void persists.

Abraham was a self-made man.

Abraham accumulated much wealth, but he also understood that the purpose of life is precisely to enrich oneself—materially, spiritually, intellectually and emotionally—in order to then also strive to enrich others.

To enrich oneself in order to then enrich others is what it means to lead a balanced and sagacious altruistic existence.

People who receive in order to also give to others tend to feel more internally nourished and uplifted.

Such people do not walk about life feeling constant disquiet and an underlying looming inner void.

And that's why the first spiritual commandment given to the founder of monotheism, a wealthy man, is to also strive to enrich the lives of others.

Let us walk in Abraham's light and emulate his beneficent ways, for the very quality of our inner lives depends on it.

Mentalizing Others: The Desire To Be Understood

Oprah Winfrey was arguably the most successful Talk Show host in the history of television.

When Oprah concluded her Talk Show, after decades of interviewing people from all walks of life, from billionaires and heads of state to the homeless and the utterly impoverished, Oprah was asked what she learned about the human condition.

Oprah stated that she learned that "everyone has a story, and everyone wants to be heard."

The stories that we tell each other about our lives and the world around us are known in psychology as "narratives," and the desire to be heard and understood is known in psychological quarters as the desire to be "mentalized."

Mentalizing is a courageous and imaginative emotional and intellectual leap, in which we verbally demonstrate to another person that we understand where they're mentally coming from.

When a person feels that they were adequately and accurately mentalized by the person they are speaking with, they feel like they can emotionally breathe.

They feel recognized and heard, and are then also more receptive to the views and perspectives of the second person.

Just like we see the world differently from different visual vantage points and angles, we also see the world differently given our distinct and varied biographical and cultural differences.

In the book of Exodus, the Torah challenges us "to know the soul of the stranger" (Exodus 23:9).

While the immediate context of this verse addresses knowing the soul of the politically vulnerable and the oppressed, this teaching could also be extended to also strive "to know the soul" of people who truly matter in our lives, by trying to mentalize them in their presence as best we can.

Reciprocal and effective mentalizing can save marriages and fraught relationships between parents and children, as well as siblings, other relatives, and good friends.

Effective mentalizing at the work place can lead to more tangible success, as well as the cultivation of a safer and more friendly working environment.

Politically, mentalizing our political foes can also lead the way to building future bridges of hope and reconciliation, greater understanding and empathy, as well as mutual respect.

In a word, mentalizing is an imperative psychological skill that we must cultivate and acquire if we covet healthy, functional, intimate and safe relationships with our loved ones and with anyone else who matters and has an impact on our lives.

Integrity: A Key for Mental Health

Noah Muroff is a nice Jewish boy. He is also a rabbi, and a Jewish educator.

In 2013, Noah bought a used desk on Craigslist for $150.

However, the desk didn't fit through the door into Noah's study, so Noah took the desk apart in order to get it inside.

It was then that a bag containing ninety eight thousand dollars in cash fell out of the desk.

That very day, Rabbi Muroff called the woman from whom he bought the desk, and told her that he found the money.

The woman sobbed, and told the rabbi that this money was part of her inheritance.

The next day, Rabbi Muroff, who teaches ninth grade in a yehisvah in New Haven, took his four kids along, and returned the money to its rightful owner.

In the book of Exodus, the Torah stipulates that the ark containing the Ten Command-ments should be covered with pure gold from the outside and also from within.

In the Talmud, the sages are puzzled as to why the ark should also be covered with pure gold from the inside, after all—nobody gets to see the ark from within.

The answer given by the Talmud is that this is a symbolic teaching, in order to convey to us that a person of integrity should be golden inside out.

No doubt, the story of rabbi Noah Muroff and the money he returned to its rightful owner is a clear case of a person of impeccable integrity who is golden inside out.

In the early 1980's, psychologist Steven Hayes developed a novel psychological modality known as Acceptance and Commitment Therapy (ACT).

As a psychological modality, ACT places prime importance upon my commitment to actualizing and living inside out my values and ideals in life.

ACT essentially postulates that cultivating integrity and alignment between my values and my actions is a vital component of mental health.

People who are golden inside out, people who cultivate a congruence between their inner ideals and their external deeds, such people are also at times the beneficiaries of robust mental health as a consequence.

I have never seen a closer relationship between ethics and mental health.

Right before his death, Rabbi Yochanan Ben Zakay blessed his disciples that they should fear Heaven as much as they fear a fellow human being who is merely flesh and blood.

In other words, Rabbi Ben Zakay is hailing people of integrity, those who do the right thing even when no other human being is looking at them.

Right before Jews recite the holiest prayer of the year on Yom Kippur—Kol Nidrey, we recite a verse from psalm 97, which states: "Light is sown to the righteous, and those who have an honest disposition know veritable joy."

Rabbi Noah Muroff knows veritable joy.

It is the kind of joy which radiates inside out, from strength of character and sacred naïveté.

I envy Rabbi Muroff's children who went along with their father in the car to return the money to its rightful owner.

For these children are blessed with a parent who models not only true piety, but also—immeasurable inner reservoirs of integrity and mental health.

The Third Love: Humanizing Others

In 2011, Rabbi Jonathan Sacks delivered an invocation prayer in the US Senate.

In this prayer, Rabbi Sacks implored us to remember "that the people not like us are still people, like us."

This is not always easy to recall and uphold.

In times of deadly conflict with radical and pernicious evil forces who overtly seek our destruction, the heart can easily be sealed off and hermetically sealed and locked when confronted with the acute suffering of the innocent other.

In Judaism, the servitude and de-humanization which we underwent in Egypt serves a distinct pedagogical purpose.

The subjugation in Egypt, insists the Torah, was akin to an "iron furnace," which molded our national character as a compassionate and humane culture.

Ideally, the enslavement in Egypt was a sustained tutorial in weaning humanity from the ferocious notion that someone else's humanity is in any way lesser than my own.

In this context, it is striking it that the Torah wants us to "know the soul of the stranger" (Exodus 23:9).

In other words, the Torah is asking us to take an imaginative leap, and to uphold multiple perspectives.

The Torah is challenging us to psychologically "mentalize" other human groups, to empathically behold life as experienced from the lens of other people who are not like me in terms of ethnicity, gender, faith, or lack thereof.

The two most prominent loves in the Torah are the love of God, and the love of my fellow—the love of the friend or acquaintance of mine who is like me, from my own milieu or tribe.

Surely the most demanding love, the love which calls for the suspension of deeply ingrained prejudices and stereotypes, is the third love mentioned in the Torah, the love of the stranger, the love of someone who is utterly different from me.

Once more, in the words of Rabbi Sacks, we are called upon by the Almighty to realize "that the one who is not in our image is nonetheless in God's image."

In an age infested with what Rabbi Sacks called "altruistic evil" and "pathological dualism," let us preserve and safeguard our own humanity, by remaining cognizant and sensitized to the humanity of the other.

Cathartic Speech: Telling Your Story

My paternal grandfather, Shlomo Sessler, was a Holocaust refugee.

I grew up listening to him recount the saga of his miraculous escape from the claws of Nazism time and again.

In contrast to many other survivors, my grandfather found existential catharsis in incessantly retelling the story of his flight from the looming menace of genocide and annihilation.

My grandfather was only seventeen years old when he ran for his life.

Yet unlike millions of others, who were by far his superiors in age, intellect and education, my grandfather somehow intuited and discerned that there was no physical future for the Jews of Europe under Nazi sovereignty.

Like everyone else, my grandfather did not envision gas chambers, for as Hannah Arendt observed in her magisterial "The Origins of Totalitarianism," "Normal people don't know that everything is possible."

However, my grandfather did surmise that the Germans would work the Jews of Europe to death.

With the exception of one brother, my grandfather was the sole survivor from his entire family.

In the words of the Bible, he was a "solitary branch salvaged from the all-consuming fire."

When I think about what empowered my grandfather to move on with his life, to build a family, start a business and affirm life, a verse from the book of Job comes to mind: "I shall speak, and find comfort."

For it was the constant re-narrating of his wartime saga that enabled my grandfather to come to grips with history's demons and to transform yesteryear's open wounds into an enclosed and self-contained scar.

Philosopher Alasdair McIntyre teaches us that humans are "the story-telling animal."

In other words, we construct narratives about our lives and we inhabit and experience the world through the existential lens of these epic mental constructs.

The same applied to my grandfather with regard to his wartime experiences.

It was by articulating his harrowing story of escape from genocide time and again—and to virtually anyone who would care to listen—that my grandfather was able to carry on and meet life's interminable material and psychological exigencies with vigor.

The very same psychological insight about the imperative to carry our past with us through life's manifold journeys—as painful as that carrying may be—is inherent in the Torah portion of Ki Tisa.

This Torah portion includes the story of the shattering of the Ten Commandments by Moses after the sordid idolatrous fiasco of the Golden Calf.

Later on in the Torah, in the book of Deuteronomy, the two sets of tablets with the Ten Commandments are mentioned again: the first set—which was shattered by Moses—and the second set—which remained integrated and intact.

In the Talmud, the rabbis deliberate as to which of the two sets of tablets is to be placed in the Ark of the Covenant.

Is it the second, integrated and intact set of tablets, upon which the Ten Commandments were engraved, or is it the first set, which was shattered to pieces by Moses as a spontaneous act of pietistic protestation and righteous indignation?

The sages' ingenious and poignant insight is that both the shattered set and the intact set of tablets should be placed in the ark.

This stunning midrash is both psychologically astute and existentially imperative.

It teaches us that we cannot simply bury the wounds and traumas of yesteryear; we are destined to dwell with them.

We are called upon to carry our brokenness within us throughout our life's journey, and to soulfully transition from a terrain of psychological fragmentation into a promised land of inner integration.

If we covet health, sanity, enduring mental equilibrium and robust relationships with loved ones, we are to carry our brokenness in the ark of human consciousness and integrate it into the tumultuous sagas of our life-stories.

Carry your brokenness and articulate it, implore us the Talmudic sages.

For the alternative to integrating your brokenness into your life's journey is a chronic and pervasive mental injury, a wounded soul.

Self-Care: The Choreography of Everyday Life

If somebody were to ask you what is the most important verse in the entire Torah, what would you say?

This precise question is actually being posed in a Midrashic anthology (compilation of rabbinic teachings) known as the "Ein Yaakov."

According to one rabbi, the most important verse in the entire Torah is "Shema Yisrael."

This verse epitomizes pristine monotheism and the mystical insight that all entities exist within the infinity of God.

No doubt, Shema Yisrael is indeed a cornerstone verse in Jewish theology.

According to a second rabbi, the most seminal verse in the entire Torah is the verse stipulating that God created humanity in God's image.

No doubt, this is also a foundational verse, carrying incalculable political and moral ramifications.

For the notion that we are all of equal and intrinsic worth before God ultimately paved the path to modern-day democracy and human rights.

Thirdly, another rabbi proposes that the most central verse in the entire Torah is Leviticus 19:18, which includes the words "Love your fellow person as yourself."

To be sure, this verse also conveys to us a chief facet of the human condition—the foundational psychological insight that we should empathize with other people, put ourselves in their shoes, and treat them in the exact same way that we would like to be treated ourselves.

Finally, a fourth rabbi offers a fourth alternative as to which verse is the most important verse in the entire Torah.

This fourth rabbi points to a rather obscure and esoteric verse from the book of Numbers dealing with the intricacies of the sacrificial rites.

According to this verse, one should bring forth as a daily offering the first lamb in the morning, "and the second lamb during dusk."

Ultimately, the master rabbi accepts the opinion of the fourth rabbi who argues that the most important verse in the entire Torah pertains to the daily offerings of our spiritual obligations.

This surprising decision is correlated to an important principle in everyday life, namely—that those of us who methodically carry out their daily rituals of self-care in an orderly and disciplined fashion reap handsome existential dividends.

For example, the late novelist Amos Oz used to start every day of his life with an hour-long walk in the Judean desert.

After this physical exercise, which was also a spiritual contemplative practice which empowered Amos Oz to "keep a perspective on eternity" in his own words, Oz would ceremoniously enjoy his morning coffee with a modest and light breakfast, and then finally "open shop" as an author and start his daily craft of writing.

Excellence, observed Aristotle, "is not a virtue, but a habit."

Those of us who habitually physically and spiritually exercise on a daily basis succeed in the fine and imperative art of self-care and general well-being.

And that's why the Torah verse about bringing forth our daily offerings promptly, with precision and disciplinary exactitude, is considered such a prime Jewish teaching-because it conveys to us the timeless insight that health and overall existential well-being are contingent upon rigorous and consistent daily practices known in psychology as ADL's—activities of daily living.

Maintaining Boundaries

As an Israeli child, whenever we traveled down south along the border between Israel and Jordan, I would observe transfixed the close proximity of the cars driving on the Jordanian side of the border.

The enemy seemed so physically close, but culturally, politically and psychologically—the enemy was light years away and utterly removed from us.

There was a staggering dissonance between the minuteness of the physical distance and the enormity of the political distance between Israel and its former enemy.

Parshat Shmini, the third Torah portion in the book of Leviticus, is all about maintaining and respecting boundaries.

The colossal failure of two of Aaron's sons who perished on account of sacrificing an enigmatic "foreign fire," had to do with disrespecting boundaries.

According to one commentary, the brothers did not respect familial and inter-generational boundaries, by not adhering to the seniority of the elders—Aaron and Moses.

According to another interpretation, the brothers deviated from the legalistic stipulation, and brought forth a forbidden offering.

Whether Aaron's sons' transgression was familial, legal, spiritual or moral, clearly theirs was a failure to maintain and respect boundaries.

In order to live well, we need to assertively maintain our own boundaries on the one hand, and not encroach upon another person's boundaries on the other hand.

Judaism is a sustained tutorial in maintaining and respecting boundaries.

Whether it is the dietary boundaries stipulated later on in the parshah, or the suspension of technology on Shabbat, or the refraining from bread on Passover and the fasting on seminal days, Rabbi Soloveitchik observed that in Judaism we also know how to surrender before the divine by respecting sacred boundaries.

Delayed gratification and respect of inner psychological boundaries are an a-priori for mental and emotional health.

Without psychological boundaries there is no sanity, and in the absence of socio-political boundaries there is chaos instead of order, anarchy in lieu of the rule of law, and nihilism instead of meaning.

From Shame To Guilt: Judaism's Moral Evolution

The Torah portions of Tazria-Metzorah are well-known for their esotericism and obscurity.

These two Torah portions, which are usually read together, chiefly deal with an ancient physical condition known as "tzara'at."

The sages of antiquity labored hard to excavate spiritual and moral meanings from these two Torah portions.

The rabbis offered the insight that the Hebrew word "tzara'at" is etymologically correlated to the Hebrew term מוציא שם רע, which is about engaging in vile speech about other people.

Thus, for the ancients, the condition of tzara'at was spiritual retribution for engaging in vile speech.

Another way of looking at tzara'at has to do with the human psychological phenomenon of shame.

Shame has to do with a negative outlook about what we think or feel that other people are thinking about us.

The individuals who were afflicted with tzara'at had to deal with the shame inherent in the pervasive visibility of their condition.

For the Torah states that this condition appeared on people's homes, furniture, skin, hair and garments, which was a source of embarrassment and shame for them.

Anthropologist Ruth Benedict famously distinguished between shame cultures and guilt cultures.

At its best, Judaism is a guilt culture, and not a shame culture.

In shame cultures, people are fearful of external social perceptions of their comportment, whereas guilt cultures are more internally focused and have to do with a sense of inner culpability and conscience.

The Torah starts its narrative with guilt and shame—the guilt of Adam and Eve having eaten from the tree of knowledge, and the shame that Adam and Eve experienced after they became conscious of their nakedness.

Yom Kippur, the holiest day of the Jewish year, is about internal introspective pondering of guilt.

Indeed, the communal confession articulated on Yom Kippur starts with the word אשמנו, which means "we were guilty."

On fast days in which we commemorate historical catastrophes, we express in the liturgy the perspective that it is "on account of our own misdeeds that we were exiled" from the land of Israel.

Judaism is a religion of radical responsibility, and responsibility necessitates self-scrutiny and honest introspection of our deeds and misdeeds.

By moving away from shame culture to guilt culture, Judaism contributed to the overall evolution of Western civilization as a whole from external social sanctions to inner judgment in the sacred chamber of one's innermost heart.

As we examine our own failings, let us also be more focused on guilt rather than on shame, on conscience rather than on external social perceptions.

The Examined Life

Rabbi Lord Jonathan Sacks always felt that he was living on borrowed time, and that he would probably die at a very young age.

In the words of his middle child, Dina Sacks, "He always knew that he was running out of time, not believing that he would live past the age of forty."

Rabbi Sacks saw the angel of death eye-to-eye four times in his life.

In his early twenties, he almost drowned to death on his honeymoon in Italy.

In his thirties, the rabbi's first battle with cancer took place, a battle from which he recovered once again in his fifties, and to which he defiantly succumbed at the beginning of his eighth decade.

It is striking and noteworthy that another towering rabbinic sage whom we lost that very same year (2020), the late Rabbi Adin Steinsaltz, also struggled with ill health throughout his entire life, and was thus also intimately acquainted with the rapidly ticking clock of human existence.

Souls such as Rabbi Sacks and Rabbi Steinsaltz are endowed with acute and pristine existential lucidity.

They constantly remember and remind themselves that our brief sojourn as living beings on this earth is a mere handful of decades, after which "we are speedily gone, and fly away (Psalm 90)."

Like President Kennedy, whose favorite poem was Alan Seeger's "I have a Rendezvous with Death," and like Steve Jobs, who counterintuitively saw death as "the single best invention of life," we should all ponder, from time to time, how we are spending our hurried sojourn on this earth, which the psalmist poetically depicts as a mere "fleeting shadow" upon the face of eternity.

In the Torah portion of "Aharey Mot," which literally means "After the Death of," The word "death," in various renditions, appears no less than three times in the opening two verses of our parshah.

Although the parshah is specifically alluding to the deaths of Nadav and Avihu, it also provides an instructive tutorial in spiritual prudence and existential accountability to us all.

It is not mere coincidence that the sages of old codified reading this Torah portion on Yom Kippur, the holiest day of the year, a day of profound spiritual reckoning, during which we observe a radical suspension of our worldly activities in order to engage in methodic self-scrutiny.

We read "Aharey Mot" both during the morning and afternoon services of Yom Kippur, thereby re-sensitizing ourselves to our looming mortality.

We do so because in the words of Socrates, "the unexamined life is not worth living."

No modern thinker was more attuned to our looming mortality than Martin Heidegger.

In his philosophical masterpiece, "Being and Time," Heidegger argued that humanity spends the bulk of its time and resources desperately striving to flee and suppress our "Being-Toward-Death."

According to Heidegger, this denial of death, which breeds an inauthentic and shallow existence, manifests itself in superficial talk about the lives of others ("idle chatter" in Heidegger's words), and in our compulsive and cowardly attempts to impress "The They," the invisible societal gaze of relatively marginal people in our lives.

The problem with suppressing our sheer finitude and temporality, implies Heidegger, is that it severs us from the profundity of our soul and from the sacred murmur of our untarnished inner core.

In Israel, when a funeral procession commences, the officiating clergy recites the following teaching from Ethics of the Fathers: "Know from whence you originate (from a drop of seed), where you are physically heading (to a place of dust, where worms consume the flesh), and before whom are you going to give spiritual accountability (before the Holy Blessed One)."

Sooner or later, all of us will hear the very same haunting existential query which God-Almighty posed to Adam in the Garden of Eden, namely—"Ayekah/Where are you?"

Two superior minds of Sephardic Jewish ancestry, French essayist Michel de Montaigne and philosopher Jacques Derrida, both argued that the task of philosophy is "to learn how to die."

Judaism, by way of contrast, is a sacred and sustained tutorial in learning how to live.

But learning how to live also necessitates, from time to time, spiritually pondering the brevity of time at our disposal, at various critical junctures and intervals during the Jewish calendarial canon.

The reading of "Aharey Mot" on Yom Kippur is certainly one of these opportune and designated spiritual times.

Make sure you show up for it in both body and soul.

Life As a Calling

Ever since my adolescence, I intuited that there must be more to life than the material dimension of human existence.

That the human story is about so much more than what Karl Marx called "Homo faber"—the human being as the producing and manufacturing animal.

This deep-seated intuition, that there's more to life than the race for income, was factually and empirically corroborated for me back in 2006.

During that year, the General Social Survey in the United States revealed some astounding findings about what the Dalai Lama called "the art of happiness."

The survey found that the practitioners of the following professions reported the highest rates of career satisfaction in their work: clergy, educators, nurses, fire fighters, artists and therapists.

What do all these professions have in common?

They are all about so much more than "making a living." Rather, they are about elevating and enhancing the lives of others.

Many of us are brainwashed from our very childhood by the market economy ethos that inner contentment is to be achieved by pursuing professions which carry exceptionally high monetary dividends.

But as Albert Einstein wisely observed, "not everything that counts can be counted."

Existential satiation, implies the general social survey mentioned above, is to be derived by having a sense of a calling in life, by cultivating a constant inner striving to contribute to the well-being of others and the overall advancement of human welfare.

This germane existential insight about the inherent connection between altruism and happiness is exemplified in the very opening word of the book of Leviticus in the Torah.

That word is "Vayikra," which means "Called upon."

Usually, when God allegorically addresses Moses in the Torah, the text uses the word "Vaydaber" ("And God spoke") or "Vayomer ("And God said").

So why is it that the opening word of the Torah book discussing sacrifices depicts God as "calling upon" Moses, rather than God merely "saying" to Moses, or "speaking" to Moses?"

One reason for that is that the Torah is addressing here the universal Moses lurking within each and every one of us.

The Torah is alluding here to the pristine altruistic streak inherent in every human soul.

We are all being existentially summoned and challenged here.

We are all "called upon" by a cosmic voice, which is also an inner voice, to see life not only as a solipsistic socio-economic endeavor, but also as a sacred altruistic vocation.

If you feel a little under the weather, a wise relative advised me once, then "go and volunteer."

For few things in life enhance and invigorate the human spirit more than the knowledge that you are useful, relevant and helpful to those around you.

That you truly make a difference in people's lives, and that you lead an impactful existence by enriching and beautifying the lives of others.

In the words of Rabbi Hillel in the Talmud "the rest is commentary," now go and "be a blessing" (Genesis 12:2).

Emotional Intelligence: What God Expects of Us

In his groundbreaking book "Emotional Intelligence," Daniel Goleman defines emotional intelligence as "the ability to identify and regulate one's emotions, and understand the emotions of others."

Connecting the dots emotionally and knowing why we feel what we feel is a highly evolved psychological level.

In the book of Genesis, the patriarch Jacob exemplifies emotional intelligence.

When Jacob is overcome with fear before his encounter with his brother Esau (Genesis 32:8), he recognizes the intensity of his feelings, and therefore regroups and divides his household and entourage into two distinct units.

Here Jacob was able to identify and regulate his own emotions by recognizing them and acting in a way that could decrease them.

Earlier in the text, Jacob also notices a changed expression on his uncle Laban's face (Genesis 31:2).

Here Jacob subtly notices the body language of his uncle, and understands that it is indicative of an emotional change.

Jacob/Israel is the spiritual namesake of the entire Jewish people.

To be a spiritual descendant of Jacob/Israel thus also entails being endowed with emotional intelligence as defined by Dr. Goleman—the ability to recognize and regulate my own emotions and also be sensitized and attuned to other people's feelings.

For Daniel Goleman, EQ (emotional intelligence) "can matter more than IQ"—more than intellectual intelligence—as far as our overall existential success is concerned.

Jewish culture is a culture of hyper-literacy and ultra-intellectualism.

Ours is a culture which sanctifies and hails the depth and pathos of the written word and the power of ideas.

May we also grow in soul as individuals, such that we can further be a blessing to the world as emotionally intelligent beings who are aware of their own feelings and sensitized to the emotive states of other people.

Sages of the Heart: Beyond Empathy

Rabbi Chaim of Brisk was a towering Talmudic sage.

He was also endowed with a compassionate and caring heart.

It is said that one day a woman came to see Rabbi Chaim shortly before Passover, and asked the rabbi a question in Jewish law.

The woman's question was whether one can drink milk instead of wine during the Passover Seder.

The rabbi didn't verbally respond to the woman's question. He simply took out all the cash in his wallet and gave it to her.

For Rabbi Chaim was not only an intellectual sage, he was also a sage of the heart, and instantaneously understood the woman's predicament.

Rabbi Chaim figured out that if the woman is asking him about drinking milk during the Passover Seder, then she obviously cannot afford to buy meat, as it is forbidden in the Jewish tradition to consume meat and dairy products together.

In the book of Exodus, the Torah offers a beautiful term for those who are imbued with divine wisdom and a special know-how (Exodus 28:3).

The Torah calls such outstanding individuals חכמי לב, which means: "Sages of the heart."

In his groundbreaking book "Emotional Intelligence," psychologist Daniel Goleman defines emotional intelligence as the ability to recognize and regulate my own emotions, as well as the ability to understand the emotions of other people.

The Torah goes a step further than Dr. Goleman.

For the Torah, a sage of the heart is able not only to understand the emotions of another person, but also to anticipate their needs ahead of time—like Rabbi Chaim did in the story about the woman who came to ask him about drinking milk during the Passover Seder.

In an ideal world, we would all strive to be sages of the heart.

A sage of the heart is akin to a professional waiter who is always on guard, waiting to see if there is anything that the people sitting around the table might want or need.

In a liturgical poem known as "Yigdal," Jews sing every Friday night about God as the one who is צופה ויודע סתרינו, the One who anticipates and observes that which is concealed, that which is not yet verbalized.

Such is the inner quality of the sages of the heart—they observe ahead of time that which had not yet even been articulated or explicitly asked for.

A sage of the heart is also akin to a chess player who sees several steps ahead in the intricate and subtle chessboard of human relationships.

We often hail empathy—the ability to understand the feelings of another person, as a seminal emotive quality.

Anticipating ahead of time what a person actually needs goes a level beyond that.

I was once blessed to have a 97 year old congregant who was a highly active and exceptionally contributive member of the community.

The congregant's voicemail greeting summarized what it means to be a sage of the heart.

This man's voicemail greeting stated the following words:

> "My name is Hy Arnesty. If there is anything I can do for you, please let me know. Thank you."

Like the professional waiter who eagerly awaits to detect a client's need or request, like an ingenious chess player who anticipates that which will occur soon thereafter, Hy Arnesty was the personification of what it truly means to be a sage of heart.

May we walk in his light, and emulate his ways, such that we too can become a blessing to the world, and give spiritual pleasure to our Parent in heaven.

Competitiveness: The Antithesis of Jewish Spirituality

A few years ago, my daughter participated in a Spelling Bee competition.

She did very well.

This year my daughter decided not to participate in the Spelling Bee competition, and I am very happy about it.

I never competed intellectually with anyone, and I don't believe in competing with other people in an academic setting.

Growing up, I always had very mediocre grades. I simply didn't care about it.

I was too busy reading books which were not part of the school curriculum.

In the ingenious words of Mark Twain: "I have never allowed my schooling to interfere with my education."

Vincent Van Gogh, Albert Einstein and William Shakespeare did not compete with other people in their respective fields.

They competed internally, with their own God-given inner potential, and that holds true with regard to most highly creative and groundbreaking thinkers and artists.

Haman, the villain of the Purim story, was a very competitive person.

Many people don't necessarily notice it, but the source of Haman's murderous enmity towards the Jewish people, and also his subsequent political demise and untimely death, were all a direct consequence of his chronic psychological insecurity, of the fact that he obsessively competed with other people for political hegemony.

In a striking passage in the book of Esther (5:13), Haman confides in his wife, and tells her that all his manifold political achievements are simply "not worth it," on account of Mordechai sitting at the King's gate, and enjoying a more prominent position than he, Haman, does.

To be sure, competitive sport certainly has its place—it is entertaining, and it can also be exhilarating and exciting.

In the business world and in politics as well, we inevitably compete for power and wealth, as these are scarce resources.

But in the inner domain of the spirit, at the deepest of levels, our ultimate success is internal rather than external, it is metaphysical rather than tangible.

In their book "Raising A+ Human Beings," educators Bruce Powell and Ron Wolfson beseech us to cultivate a new educational culture, one which is less obsessed with grades, and more focused on cultivating character traits and values.

This approach is highly commensurate with the age-old Jewish approach to academic Torah study "lishmah"—which means rigorous and demanding intellectual study intrinsically and for its own sake, for the sheer spiritual joy and inner fulfillment inherent in the learning process itself.

May we all be blessed with parents and schools who inspire young people to learn intrinsically and lishmah, so that they can truly be empowered to grow in soul and become a source of blessing to society at large.

Confronting Anxiety: Beyond Inner Captivity

Steve Hayes is a world-class psychologist.

He is also a brave and tormented man.

In his TED talk, Steve Hayes courageously revealed that he suffers from chronic panic attacks.

One of Steve Hayes' panic attacks was so severe that he actually rushed himself to the ER thinking that he was getting a heart attack.

As a result of his panic attacks, Steve Hayes developed a new and powerful way to confront anxiety and observe his anxiety from the outside.

Hayes' method of confronting anxiety is part of a psychological modality that he developed.

The name of this psychological modality is ACT, and it stands for Acceptance and Commitment Therapy.

The "Acceptance" part of this modality has to do with accepting the inevitability of difficult and painful feelings when they hit us.

Anxiety is one of the most common types of mental struggles, and about one out of five Americans are affected by it each year.

Steve Hayes' way of approaching his own anxiety and panic disorder is reflective of an insight which appears in the book of Job: "I shall speak and find comfort" (32:20).

According to Steve Hayes, the way to decrease and tame anxiety is simply to verbalize it with curiosity as an outside observer.

For example, Hayes could say to himself: "I am noticing that I am feeling anxious right now, because I have a pressing deadline at work."

Noticing our feelings as an outside observer reminds us that a fleeting feeling is not intrinsic to who we are.

It could also potentially lower the flame and intensity of the debilitating feeling.

By expressing out loud and with words difficult and painful feelings we can decrease their efficacy, and become more aware of their root cause.

This is a powerful and effective way to decrease the intensity of an emotion, and to learn how to dwell with it until it passes.

It is possible to think of painful feelings as a nasty roommate.

Eventually the nasty roommate will bid us farewell and leave the apartment of our inner world.

But the nasty roommate will also come back at some point to revisit us, and then eventually unceremoniously leave us once more.

Our biblical ancestors were no strangers to heart-wrenching anxiety.

In the Torah, Isaac experiences anxiety (חרדה), after Isaac realizes that he gave Jacob the blessing that he intended for Esau (Genesis 27:33).

In the book of Jeremiah (30:5), the prophet proclaims that in calamitous times we hear the "voice of fear/anxiety," and in the book of Daniel the people fled after "great anxiety befell them" (10:7).

There is simply no way to exist in this world in the absence of painful and at times even debilitating emotions.

One thing we can do is to make temporary peace with a challenging feeling, make room for it, accept its fleeting presence, express it, and lean on others, until it eventually leaves us alone and goes away.

Self-Fullness: Between Giving and Receiving

Rabbi Simcha Bunim of Peshischa was a towering Chassidic sage.

According to this sage, a person should carry two metaphorical notes in each pocket.

One note should read: "I am but ashes and dust," and the second note should read: "The world was created for my sake."

In other words, between the polarity of selfishness ("the world was created for my sake"), and a life of utter selflessness and self-negation ("I am but ashes and dust")—there lies a harmonizing middle path.

This middle path represents the moderating approach of "Self-fullness," in which we strive to achieve that ever-elusive balance between giving and receiving.

Maimonides, following Aristotle, advocated pursuing the middle path of moderation in virtually all human affairs.

In the Kabbalah, the biblical figure of Jacob personifies the spiritual attribute of "Tifereth." Tifereth means "exquisite beauty."

Tifereth is the moderating and intermediating sefirah (divine attribute) between Chessed and Gevurah/Din, between unconditional love and boundless giving on the one hand, and self-constriction and the exercise of rigorous discipline on the other hand.

In Judaism, we reject the dichotomous polarities of utter selfishness on the one hand, and radical self-effacement on the other hand.

We walk with Maimonides and the medieval Kabbalists, who knew the cherished and ennobling middle path of the ultimate give-and-take, the give-and-take exemplified by the spirit of self-fullness.

Gratitude: The Antidote to Envy

Joseph's brothers were envious of his prodigious gifts. They also envied the special love that Jacob harbored towards Joseph.

As we know, their envy was so ferocious that they literally contemplated murdering their own brother, whom they ultimately sold to slavery.

In the Bible, in the Song of Songs, King Solomon states that envy is as ferocious as the inferno.

In the Mishnah, the sages postulate that envy is one of those heinous dispositions that can literally remove a person from the world.

In other words, a person can become so engrossed by ruminative envy, to the extent that it robs this person of their presence of mind to attend to other facets of their life.

The best antidote to destructive envy is gratitude.

Famously, the first two words a Jew is summoned to utter upon waking up are "Modeh Ani," which means—"Grateful Am I."

Notice that the word "Grateful" precedes the word "I" in the Hebrew. "Grateful" is literally the first word we are invited to articulate as we start our day.

In the immortal words of Rabbi Sacks זצ״ל: "We thank before we think."

Envy is a double-edged sword.

In the case of spiritual envy, it can serve as a positive catalyst for the cultivation of more refined qualities such as wisdom, kindness and benevolence.

Conversely, when it comes to tangible goods, envy can turn into a demonic obsession.

In such cases, to be sure, gratitude for the plentitude and abundance that what we already possess constitutes the most efficacious antidote to the curse and malady of boundless envy.

Beyond Resilience:
Jacob's Existential Excellence

The story of Jacob dislocating the socket of his hip as he struggled with an enigmatic stranger in the dead of night epitomizes the human spiritual capacity to grow beyond mere resilience.

Resilience means that I remain intact and unscathed following an external challenge. That I retain and preserve my original state of being despite pressure and adversity.

Going beyond mere resilience is a hallmark feature of the Jewish condition. We not only persevere, we soar from brokenness.

Brokenness is what gave rise to the creation of the cosmos according to the Kabbalistic cosmology of the broken vessels.

According to the Talmud, the brokenness of the original set of the Ten Commandments was preserved in the Arc of the Covenant, precisely in order to teach us about the redemptive virtue of growing and healing beyond brokenness.

The Torah states that Jacob arrived back in Israel physically intact, as an "ish shalem", an integrated person.

According to Rashi, this means that Jacob healed from the injury incurred earlier during the nocturnal struggle.

Human biology teaches us that muscles tear before they grow. The same holds with regard to the human spirit.

This is exemplified by the Japanese art of Kintsugi, in which we paint broken pottery pieces together with gold. This exquisite art form symbolizes, beyond its aesthetic virtues, the ability to redeem and beautify our own internal brokenness.

Redeeming our inner brokenness is precisely what Israel, our ancestral spiritual namesake achieved, when he arrived back in Israel as an integrated and wholesome person.

And this is also what we, at our finest moments, have been teaching the world ever since.

From Helplessness to Hopefulness: Judaism & Post Traumatic Growth

The binding of Isaac is the most dramatic story in the entire Torah.

In this story, Abraham, following a divine command, ties the hands and feet of his son Isaac, and takes out a knife to slaughter him.

At the last moment, an angel intercedes and orders Abraham to desist from killing his own son.

It is plausible to argue that Isaac may have developed what modern psychology calls "post-traumatic stress," as a result of this dramatic near death experience orchestrated by the hands of his own father.

The dialogue between Abraham and Isaac prior to the binding of Isaac is the last recorded dialogue between father and son in the entire Torah, and a dramatic rupture may well have ensued between them.

Isaac then grows up to become a highly introverted soul. Unlike his father and his own sons, Isaac never leaves Israel, and also gets married later in life.

But eventually, Isaac recuperates and bounces back.

Later on, the Torah describes Isaac as meditating in the field, which according to the Talmud means that Isaac was spiritually innovative and resilient, and that he established the afternoon prayer service.

After that, Isaac also finds comfort in marrying Rebecca, and in raising children. He is blessed with emotional intimacy, and with service to others as a caring and loving parent.

Lastly, later on in life, Isaac also endeavors to dig deep and find new water sources, which according to the mystical commentators means that Isaac became a spiritual trailblazer and devised novel spiritual paths, that he found his own unique voice in life, and left an imprint on the world.

On all these levels, it is clear that Isaac exhibited what Martin Seligman, the Jewish-American founder of positive psychology calls "post traumatic growth."

Isaac ultimately emerged from his traumatic binding spiritually fortified, emotionally enriched, and existentially enhanced.

Isaac is the father of Israel, after whom the entire Jewish nation is named.

The story of Isaac is thus inspirational for all of us to grow through adversity and heartache the way our ancestor did, the way the father of Israel exemplifies for all of us to be.

Emotional Maturity:
Beyond Splitting

The Torah portion of Metzorah deals with ritual purity.

For most Jews today, ritual purity no longer holds such a central place in their religious practice, but emotional purity still remains a seminal striving of the Jewish spiritual condition.

On Shabbat, we implore God twice during the prayer service to "purity our heart," and in psalm 51 we beseech God to fashion for us "a pure heart."

Emotional purity is about being able to behold other people in a favorable light, or in the words of the Mishnah "to judge every person favorably."

The Lubavitcher Rebbe used to say that people dress up in various costumes all year long, and not only during the Jewish holiday of Purim.

During the rest of the year too, argued the Rebbe, some people habitually "dress up" as grumpy, ungrateful, rude or embittered.

But deep inside, implied the Rebbe, most of these people also have some redeeming qualities, and not only deficiencies and shortcomings.

The founder of the Chassidic movement, the Ba'al Shem Tov, also insisted that we should focus on other people's positive attributes.

In psychology, Ronald Fairbairn introduced the cognitive distortion known as "splitting."

Splitting entails emotional black and white thinking in which we either idealize a certain person and see them as perfect, or demonize that very same person, and see them as intrinsically evil.

As mere mortals, we cannot really obtain full-fledged emotional purity, but we can still achieve, with time and effort, a high measure of emotional maturity.

Emotional maturity requires subtlety and the ability to avoid splitting, by seeing other people three dimensionally, and in a balanced and nuanced way.

"The Merciful One [God] desires the heart," teaches us the Talmud (Sanhedrin 106B).

Surely, the heart that the Almighty desires for us to acquire is a mature and nuanced heart.

It is also a heart which is compassionately attuned to the tensions and contradictions inherent in the human condition.

Overcoming Grief/Making Meaning After Loss

In the Torah, Sarah dies after a traumatic family event.

Abraham then goes on "to eulogize Sarah, and to cry for her."

Eulogizing and crying are two very different things.

When we cry for someone, we allow ourselves to emotionally process our sadness and grief.

When we eulogize someone, we pay loving tribute to them, and even celebrate their virtues and loving contributions to the world.

In Hebrew, the word "why" is pronounced "lama," and the words "what for" are pronounced as "lema."

In Hebrew, the word for "why" and the words "what for" are the same word, which is spelled as למה.

This teaches us that after we experience a devastating loss, we can either ask למה as in "why?" or למה as in "what for?"

There is no human answer as to the question "why" did a particular tragedy occur.

But "what for" is the life-affirming Jewish response to untimely death and devastating loss.

Abraham harnessed Sarah's death to embark upon proactive life-affirming endeavors such as acquiring land in Israel and finding a suitable spouse for his son.

Rona Ramon, who lost both her husband and her son in tragic accidents, personified the Jewish resilient approach of למה as in "what for."

After losing both her husband and her son, Rona Ramon became a holistic therapist thereby teaching people how to deal with bereavement and loss.

May we follow in the spiritual footsteps of Abraham and Rona Ramon by allowing ourselves to first mourn the death of a loved one, and after that to also strive to perpetuate their memory in a life-affirming and meaningful way.

Unconditional Love:
A Godly Quality

In the Torah portion of Behookotay, God promises the Jewish people that they are an eternal people, and that God will never annihilate the Jewish nation no matter how egregious their misdeeds may be.

God's pledge to uphold His relationship with the Jewish people no matter the circumstances comes as close as the Torah gets to the concept of unconditional love.

The concept of unconditional love is intrinsic to the parent-child relationship.

For a child, parental unconditional love is part and parcel of emotional safety, the feeling that the child is seen as of worth and accepted, despite their shortcomings and flaws.

Similarly, psychologist Carl Rogers spoke of "unconditional positive regard" in family settings, as well as in the therapeutic relationship.

In "Man's Search for Meaning," psychiatrist Viktor Frankl argued that love enables a person to fulfill their inner potential, and actualize themselves in the world.

The love that parents harbor towards their children is the closest that mere mortals can approach the kind of love that the Almighty harbors towards all of humanity.

No one captured this truth better than Rabbi Jonathan Sacks, who did well to observe that "unconditional love is not uncritical, but it is unbreakable. That is how we should love our children—for it is how God loves us."

Alienation: Overcoming Emotional Estrangement

The Torah is replete with warnings about impending national exile, should the Israelites lose their spiritual and moral compass.

Exile is not only a geo-political condition in which an individual or a nation reside outside their homeland.

Exile can also be the emotional and mental anguish of a person who is severed from their inner core.

Karl Marx wrote about alienation in the modern work place, and Albert Camus addressed alienation as a spiritual and moral condition in secular society.

The word "alienation" means estrangement, and it is about the condition of feeling like a foreigner in my own skin and social environment.

The antidotes to alienation as emotional estrangement include community, spiritual practice, deep interpersonal relationship with friends and loved ones, and an overall sense of meaning and belongingness in our lives.

Alienation as existential estrangement can give rise to a sense of overall apathy, depression and loneliness.

The best remedy to alienation is love and care.

Throughout their turbulent and tempestuous history, the Jewish people were exiled and expelled from countless countries more than any other nation in history.

However, Jews did not fall prey to alienation as an inner state of estrangement in the world.

Wherever Jews settled, they established communal networks of support and solidarity. They supported each other emotionally, spiritually and socio-economically, and were imbued with a sense of purpose and a national vocation.

The social and spiritual capital of Jewish communities sustained their spirits in a hostile and uncertain world.

Today the secular West lost much of the conditions which make for social robustness and spiritual and emotional cohesion.

Families become smaller and more fragmented, and traditional communities are imploding and shrinking.

In addition, many people don't feel that they are a part of a purpose and a cause greater than themselves, and life is reduced to the role one plays in the global market economy.

As sociologist Robert Putnam demonstrates in his book "Bowing Alone," Americans spend less and less time involved in social and communal projects and structures.

Alienation is almost synonymous with the modern urban condition.

It is hard for contemporary societies to replicate in an age of information technology the kind of social networks of support that we possessed as traditional societies.

One of the best ways to combat alienation is to become part of something greater than yourself, thereby engaging in what Martin Seligman called "the meaningful life."

People who volunteer for the common good, regularly attend social and communal gatherings, and engage in consistent spiritual practices with others, report higher degrees of happiness and life satisfaction. In a word, they are less alienated and isolated.

We have gained much from the adventure of modernity, a historical epoch whose crowning achievements include individualism, civil and human rights, and minority rights.

But somewhere along the way we lost that precarious and delicate balance between self-actualization and collective belonging, between globalism and particularism, and between the spiritual and the concrete.

If we want to avoid the kind of inner exile which the Torah and the prophets allude to in the biblical canon, we would do well to begin by finding that ever-elusive equilibrium between what Rabbi Sacks called "the I of authenticity," and the "we" of collective belonging.

Finitude: The Illusion of Ownership

There is a beautiful story about the Chafetz Chaim, a towering rabbinic sage, who lived in Europe before the Holocaust.

As the story goes, an affluent American-Jew once came to visit the rabbi in the rabbi's home, and was astounded by the austere and minimal furniture in the rabbi's home.

"Rabbi!" Exclaimed the affluent American visitor to his pious eastern European counterpart: "Where is all your stuff?"

"Where is all my stuff?" Responded the rabbi, "Where is all your stuff?"

"Me?" Retorted the astonished American, "But I'm just passing through here!"

"Me too," answered the rabbinic sage to the American visitor, "Me too, I'm also just passing through here."

We are all just passing through here in this world.

In the Torah portion of Behar, the Almighty conveys to us that we are but "strangers and sojourners" on this earth.

In other words, we are transient guests for a mere handful of decades, and the illusion of ownership is but a temporary and fleeting state of affairs.

In the final analysis, all of our worldly possessions are merely on a temporary lease, and we do not take them with us when we die.

After we die, we will be remembered for what David Brooks calls our "eulogy virtues"—our character traits and ennobling acts of kindness, and not for our "resume virtues"—such as the worth of our worldly assets and formal achievements.

The task of philosophy, argued Michel de Montaigne, is "to learn how to die."

The task of Judaism is to learn how to live deeply, and living deeply also entails a sober assessment of that which is fleeting and transient, and that which endures and withstands the test of time.

Sanctifying Anger: Judaism & Righteous Indignation

In 1975, the United Nations General Assembly passed a resolution equating Zionism with racism.

By way of protestation, Chaim Herzog, Israel's ambassador to the UN, rose to the podium and ceremoniously tore the resolution text to pieces.

This undiplomatic gesture went down in history as capturing the absurd and ludicrous nature of the resolution.

Thousands of years before that, Moses reacted in a similar fashion to another fiasco—the worshipping of the golden calf by the people of Israel.

Famously, when Moses came down the mountain and saw the ancient Israelites engaged in idolatrous practices, he shattered the Ten Commandments to pieces.

Ambassador Chaim Herzog and Moses tore the document and broke the tablets respectively because they were angry.

Anger is often thought of as a negative and dangerous emotion, because we tend to associate anger with verbal or physical aggression.

To be sure, maladaptive anger is indeed destructive and uncalled for.

However, anger itself is simply a natural human emotion.

Anger is something that we sometimes feel due to what we perceive to be an injurious statement, a loss, a betrayal, or the perpetration of injustice.

When we give anger free rein we risk wreaking havoc and making potentially irrevocable mistakes.

But when we try to completely smother our anger by radically repressing it without acknowledging it at all, we risk compromising our physical and emotional health.

In the summer of 1963, Abraham Joshua Heschel sent a telegram to President Kennedy, beseeching him to "declare a state of moral emergency," in light of the struggle for civil rights.

The time has come, wrote Heschel daringly to JFK, to summon from within the inner resources of our national spirit "moral grandeur and spiritual audacity."

Heschel channeled his anger at institutionalized racism by engaging in exemplary and steadfast civic activism.

Moses and Chaim Herzog dealt with their anger by resorting to physically symbolic gestures which became ingrained in the collective memory of the nation for generations to come.

Adaptive anger can be healthy and constructive, implies Dr. Les Greenberg, the founder of emotion-focused therapy.

According to Dr. Greenberg, anger, when handled well and not dysfunctionally, "can be a very healthy emotion."

May we work hard to deal wisely with the challenging emotion of anger, and learn how to channel and express our anger in adaptive ways which ultimately empower us to heal ourselves and our relationships in constructive and life-enhancing ways.

Radical Acceptance: Making Peace With What We Cannot Change

During the last night of his life, Dr. Martin Luther King delivered his final speech.

It was a chillingly prophetic speech.

In this speech, King likened himself to the biblical figure of Moses.

Addressing an audience for the last time in his life, Dr. King stated, that he, like Moses, had seen the promised land (of racial dignity and equality).

King then went on to reassure his supporters that even though he himself will likely die young by way of political assassination, "I want you to know tonight, that we, as a people, will get to the Promised Land."

In other words, King exhibited astonishing radical acceptance as to the prospect of his imminent untimely death.

Thousands of years before that, it was Moses himself who also exhibited radical acceptance, after the Almighty informed Moses in no uncertain terms that he will not be allowed to realize his life-long dream of setting foot in the promised land.

It was a crushing blow to Moses.

For Moses, arriving in Israel was supposed to be the pinnacle moment of a lifetime of steadfast devotion to God and service to the Jewish people.

But God willed otherwise.

Rashi, Judaism's foremost biblical commentator, notes that Moses prayed no less than 515 times for the Almighty to annul the heavenly decree prohibiting Moses from entering the promised land, but to no avail.

"No person leaves this world with even half their desires fulfilled," teaches the midrash in Kohelet Rabah.

As humans, we have all experienced the crushing blows of shattered dreams, existential disappointments, and calamitous unforeseen events and developments.

In her seminal work "Radical Acceptance: Embracing Your Life With the Heart of a Buddha," Dr. Tara Brach echoes Reinhold Niebuhr's serenity prayer, which urges us to "accept the things which we cannot change."

Practicing radical acceptance enables us to prevent pain from turning into suffering, and to ultimately move forward in life.

Rabbi Y.Y. Halberstam, also known as the Tzanz Rebbe, practiced radical acceptance after his own wife and twelve children perished in the Holocaust.

With tenacity of faith, the rebbe affirmed life and went on to build a hospital, start a new family, and write voluminous Torah commentaries.

If Rabbi Halberstam managed to practice radical acceptance, then surely we too can do the same, irrespective of our own physiological, material, familial, or psychological circumstances.

For as the late Shimon Peres observed: "There are no desperate situations, there are only desperate people."

The Architecture of Self: Setting Life Goals

While running for president in 1988, George H.W. Bush spoke about "the vision thing."

"The vision thing" is one of the chief distinctions between humanity and other species.

In philosophy we use the term "telos," which means an underlying goal or objective, an ultimate destination point for which we are striving and heading.

This coming Shabbat is spiritually nicknamed "Shabbat Hazon," which means the "Shabbat of Vision," on account of the vision of the prophet Isaiah which we commence reading this Shabbat.

Isaiah was a visionary who encouraged the people to believe in the prospect of spiritual renewal and ethical invigoration.

Isaiah reminds us that the prospect of "coming home" is indeed tenable, be it a geo-political homecoming from territorial exile, or a psycho-spiritual homecoming from an inner place of mental constriction and emotional estrangement.

Rabbi Jonathan Sacks once observed that many people spend months planning a party or a vacation, but "not a single day to plan a lifetime."

In Israel, a Jewish funeral procession starts with the officiating clergy reciting an ancient teaching which starts with the words: "Know from whence you are originating, and where you are ultimately heading."

Steven Covey, in his masterful work "The Seven Habits of Highly Effective People," wrote about the existential necessity to "begin with the end in mind,"—by which he meant to say that we should plan in advance what are our ultimate life goals on the social, familial, professional and spiritual levels.

Covey went so far as to encourage individuals to actually write down their own personal mission statements in life, in the same way that organizations and companies tend to do so nowadays.

It was Viktor Frankl who beautifully observed that "what man needs is not a tension-less state, but some goal worthy of him."

Setting life goals and working hard to attain these goals ensures that life is not only something that happens to us by forces outside our control.

In her work "The Top Five Regrets of the Dying," nurse Bronnie Ware shares that the most prevalent regret that people have on their deathbed is "I wish I'd had the courage to live a life true to myself."

One way to prevent such a tragic end of life experience is to formulate a life vision and to work hard in order to actualize that life vision, and bring it into fruition.

Ethics Before Aesthetics: A Jewish Philosophy of Beauty

In the entire Torah, only one man is described as strikingly handsome and beautiful. It is the biblical figure of Joseph.

Joseph was the son of Rachel, a woman who is also described in the Torah as stunningly beautiful.

We live in a culture which worships physical beauty.

Some of the most admired individuals in the general culture around us are physically attractive celebrities.

Physical beauty can indeed be mesmerizing and gripping.

A beautiful landscape can be soothing and cathartic. It can induce serenity and contemplation.

Beauty can be uplifting, and it can also sharpen the intellect and uplift the spirit.

It gives us joy.

In Judaism, a human face is called פנים, pronounced as "panim."

The Hebrew word for "inner," is also spelled as פנים, but it is pronounced as "pnim."

In other words, in Judaism, for beauty to be deep and authentic, the external needs to be commensurate with the internal, the physical needs to also intimate and reflect the spiritual.

When there is no congruence between the external and the internal, then that kind of beauty, in Judaism, is considered to be no more than mere facade.

In the Torah, Joseph harnessed his beauty and manifold gifts in order to nourish and sustain the lives of countless people.

Rachel, who is also described as stunningly beautiful, is the personification of empathy and a soothing and consoling presence.

Following the prophet Jeremiah, we uphold a tradition according to which it is the biblical figure of Rachel who welcomes back home the exiled and the oppressed, after year of sorrow and heartache.

I live in a city in which people spend a fortune desperately trying to cultivate a youthful and attractive physical appearance.

Ideally, the frenzy and obsession with physical beauty can also be complemented by an equally relentless pursuit of inner beauty.

Beauty of essence, which shines from within, is stronger and more enduring than physical beauty.

It is a superior kind of beauty, which does not dependent upon the affirming gaze of the human other.

Spiritual beauty is perpetual, and it remains untampered by the passage of time.

It is everlasting and deeply admirable.

It is also God-like.

Kindling Independent Flames:
The Sacred Task of Parenting

In the Torah portion of Beha'alotcha, God commands to elevate candles.

Rashi, the foremost biblical commentator, explains why the Torah uses the peculiar verb to "elevate" the candles, rather than simply to "kindle" the candles.

According to Rashi, this is because we are to kindle a candle until "the flame autonomously ascends of its accord."

In other words, when we light a candle, we only stop the lighting process once we see that the flame of the candle shines bright and strong independently of us.

The same process also holds with regard to the goal and task of parenting.

As parents, our goal is to nurture and cultivate independent souls who in the long run will be able to shine and function autonomously of us.

In psychology, according to self-determination theory, autonomy-supportive parenting promotes the child's overall well-being, and also nurtures relatedness and a robust sense of belonging.

People speak today of the "helicopter parenting," as reflective of a parent who compulsively hovers above their child and disables the child from developing vital independent tools to autonomously deal with challenges and adversity.

Children tend to leave their parental home in their late teens, in many cases in order to pursue college education elsewhere.

Our children leave us sooner than we might think.

It is therefore vital for us to train our children to develop the tools and skills necessary to shine bright and independently as much as possible, thereby also instilling in them a sense of pride, self-confidence, and overall life competence.

Intrinsic Worth: How to Build Healthy Self-Esteem

Throughout their tempestuous and volatile history, the worst and best conceivable things have been said about the Jewish people.

Louis Farrakhan called Jews "termites," and Winston Churchill called Jews "the most remarkable race which has ever appeared in the world."

Voltaire called Jews "barbarous," and Tolstoy called the Jew "a sacred being."

Hitler compared Jews to rats and roaches, and Mark Twain admirably wrote about the collective eternity of the Jewish people.

What is striking about all these dehumanizing and idealizing portraits of the Jews is that the Jewish people remained largely unaffected by these demonizations and idealizations.

When it came to external perceptions of them by other peoples, Jews largely practiced the Chassidic virtue of "hishtavoot," which means "equanimity."

Whatever the most despicable and the most admirable individuals thought of them, Jews never internalized antisemitic discourse.

The genesis of this intrinsic ability to assess one's own merits independently of societal depictions is to be found in the book of Numbers.

In the book of Numbers, a group of Jewish leaders made the fateful error of assuming that their foes saw them as mere insects, as "grasshoppers."

As a result, these individuals felt small, vincible and inferior.

This was a terrible and tragic mistake.

In actuality, the other peoples melted with fear vis a vis the prospect of an armed confrontation with the Jewish people, as became apparent later on in the book of Joshua.

Here was a clear case of the distorted and weak sense of self-appraisal which occurs when we assess our own merits based on what we think that other people are thinking about us.

Sociologist Charles Horton Cooley was never more wrong than when he postulated that "I am not what I think I am, and I am not what you think I am. I am what I think you think I am."

In an image based culture, many of us are held mentally captive and emotionally imprisoned by what we imagine that other people are thinking about us.

Jewish philosopher Alain de Botton wrote his book "Status Anxiety" about people's fears of being seen as "unsuccessful" by other people in contemporary society.

Judaism teaches that what matters mostly is methodical and authentic self-scrutiny, and making a true and honest spiritual and moral inventory of my actions and statements.

It is in the inner chambers of one's heart of hearts that we can truly discover and excavate our true self-worth.

The first chapter of the Torah contains the most revolutionary idea in the history of human thought, namely that we are all of intrinsic and infinite worth (in the divine image), irrespective of our ethnic or socio-economic attributes and circumstances.

For countless centuries, the Jewish people focused on education and social mobility irrespective of geo-political constellations.

Their story has been a sustained tutorial of how to build healthy and robust self-esteem no matter what the external perceptions may be.

This is a worthy psychological and cultural heritage for all of us to cherish and to emulate, to nurture and to keep.

Living Generously/Moving Beyond Nietzsche

Friedrich Nietzsche was the most superior atheistic mind of modern European thought.

He was also a tragically lonely and tortured soul.

Nietzsche's life was bereft of lasting intimacy or descendants.

Like Schopenhauer and Kant, his was a solipsistic and solitary existence.

Nietzsche tried to compensate for his existential inaptitude when it came to normal life, by preaching a metaphysical sermon of living beyond the dictates of the Judeo-Christian ethic.

Nietzsche advocated a novel morality for the virtuous select few, a morality which transcends the scriptural parameters of good and evil.

Tragically, Nietzsche's sister and the Nazis posthumously vulgarized his work.

But one thing remains clear.

Nietzsche was an ardent proponent of what he called "the will to power," namely— the striving of individuals to compete for dominion and power in the social arena.

According to Nietzsche, people strive to dominate others be it by aesthetic, social, political, monetary, or intellectual means.

Korach, Moses' cousin who makes a stormy appearance in the book of Numbers, is a quintessential Nietzschian figure.

Korach wanted it all.

Korach was rich, powerful and prominent. But it wasn't enough for Korach.

Korach also wanted to become the senior leader of the Jewish people.

Korach's tragic and untimely demise is symptomatic of those who are possessed by an insatiable will to power.

Nietzsche argued that we should "live dangerously." Judaism implores us to live generously.

Judaism does not deny us the human desire for self-actualization and achievement.

Judaism only qualifies these individual strivings by asserting that we should temper and moderate our worldly ambitions by seeking to also share, serve, and bestow upon others.

The purpose of life, which Korach failed to realize, is not intrinsic power for power's sake, but power for the sake of service and devotion to a cause and entity greater than oneself.

In the Mishnah, the sages caution us that a life in which we give free rein to "envy, lust and the relentless pursuit of honor," is no life at all.

This is what the story of Korach, who led a failed mutiny against Moses and Aaron, ultimately comes to teach us.

In a culture obsessed by fame, excess and egocentricity, we would all do well to temper and rein in the Korach from within.

Metamorphosis: Transforming Ourselves for the Good

Rabbi Dr. Abraham Twerski was a renowned psychiatrist whose calling in life was to work with individuals struggling with addiction.

At one point in his life, Rabbi Twerski worked with prisoners in Israeli jails who were working on bettering themselves such that they could become good citizens.

Rabbi Twerski was particularly proud of one former prisoner who returned a sizable sum of money which he found to its rightful owner.

Even people who committed heinous crimes can sometimes transform themselves and become better people and law-abiding citizens.

The children of Korach in the Torah are a clear case in point.

The sons of Korach took part in a rebellion against Moses and Aaron.

As the story goes, the earth devoured Korach and his entourage, and from the depth of the earth they all professed that Moses is truth and that Moses' Torah is truth.

What is striking about all this is the rabbinic insistence that Korach's sons ultimately changed their ways and rehabilitated themselves.

Korach's sons actually came to compose beautiful devotional psalms replete with wisdom and piety, such as psalm 49 which we recite in a house of mourning to this day.

The metamorphosis of Korach's sons from ruthless and violent self-aggrandizement to humility and piety reminds us that it is possible for us to fix our ways and better ourselves.

When it comes to Teshuvah, the Jewish spiritual imperative to self-transform for the good, it is never too late.

May we continue to better our ways until our dying day, and may we also inspire others by personal example to transform themselves for the good.

Melancholy & Epiphany: The Spirit of Vincent Van Gogh

Rav Kook was stranded in London During World War One.

The great rabbi passed his time by frequenting London's National Gallery, where he became spiritually acquainted with the masterful portraits of Rembrandt.

In his diary, Rav Kook professed that God concealed his covert divine luminous light in Rembrandt's paintings.

For me, this hidden metaphysical light is to be found in the spiritual abundance and luminous glow of Van Gogh's depictions of nature.

In the summer of 2024, I had occasion to visit the Monastery of Saint-Paul de Mausole in the French town of St. Remy de Provence.

It is in this asylum that Vincent Van Gogh was hospitalized in 1889.

As part of this visit, I had occasion to set foot in the room in which Van Gogh was institutionalized.

It was very intense and riveting, and I felt attuned to the great artist's oscillation between scarcity and abundance, between constrictive madness and overflowing genius.

Outside the monastery, sitting on a stone bench, I heard the birds hovering above the glorious lavender fields.

I believe that Van Gogh depicted the Shechinah, the immanent divine presence, with the letters of his paintbrush, and that he was overwhelmed by the sheer plentitude of his inner abundance and lucidity.

People stroll inside the monastery as if embarking upon a pilgrimage of the aesthetic and the sublime.

I felt privileged to be there, and to partake of the ambience and somber luminance of this place.

It was in Paris that I first read Irving Stone's biography of Van Gogh entitled "The Lust for Life," in which the author observes that "Vincent is not dead … his genius will go on forever … [for] he was a martyr to his love of art."

It occurred to me today that in countless offices and bureaucratic facilities around the world, one can find numerous pictures and reproductions created by Van Gogh.

I think it is done because the human soul longs for beauty even while it is encompassed by the tedious monotony of the mundane.

Van Gogh was steeped in darkness, but he also harbored luminous lights.

When I ponder Van Gogh's legacy, I am reminded of the biblical verse of Micah 7:8, in which the prophet professes: "Rejoice not my foe, for even though I may have faltered I rose up again, even though I may have dwelled in darkness—the Almighty is my light."

This latter verse is recited in some Sephardic quarters every Saturday night.

I also ponder when I think of Van Gogh the biblical verses: "And I shall turn their mourning into jubilation … and I shall gladden them from their chagrin."

The world is drenched in sadness and replete with beauty.

Let us do our fair share for the facilitation of cosmic healing for humanity, by diminishing pain and augmenting beauty in this tormented and sublime world of ours.

After all, it is for this reason, and for this reason alone, that we were created in the first place.

In other words, we are here to sanctify God's name.

Emotional Redemption: Embracing Our Mortality

The Kaddish is an ancient Jewish prayer.

It became prevalent to recite the Kaddish in memory of the deceased about a thousand years ago, following the massacre of Jewish communities in Europe during the Crusades.

The Kaddish doesn't say a single word about the dead.

The Kaddish is all about articulating aggrandizing superlatives of God's majesty, supremacy and perpetuity.

The chief psychological objective of the Kaddish is emotional redemption.

When we recite the Kaddish we become sensitized and attuned to the minuteness and briefness of a human lifespan when compared with the infinite expanses and the silent murmur of eternity.

The Kaddish is a cosmic catharsis in which we reconcile ourselves with King Solomon's existential insight in Ecclesiastes that ultimately, in the final analysis, all worldly things are destined to perish and "wither away," including our bodies and our core physicality.

By reciting the Kaddish in a communal setting, we soar beyond the mundane and find existential solace in the cosmic majesty of that which is beyond time and space.

The Kaddish is about spiritual solace and soulful invigoration.

It reminds us that man is finite, and so are his victories, and that in the end, when all is said and done, all that remains is the silent murmur of eternity, precisely as it was in the very genesis of creation, when "the spirit of God was hovering above the waters."

Sanctifying God's Name: When Religious People Serve Humanity

One of the deepest questions of our time is: "How to be religious without betraying humankind?"

We live in a time in which crimes against humanity are committed in the name of God.

During the October Seventh carnage, the perpetrators of the massacre kept on proclaiming God's greatness as they burnt, raped and beheaded.

From time immemorial, religions around the world were guilty of what Rabbi Sacks called "pathological dualism."

Pathological dualism means that I consider members of my own religious group as holy and pure, while at the same time I demonize and dehumanize members of other religions as satanic and inferior.

The Torah reading of Emor speaks about the spiritual imperative of sanctifying God's name.

To sanctify God's name in Judaism means that I serve as an ambassador of God in this world, by being an agent of hope, piety and loving-kindness in the world.

Rabbi Abraham Joshua Heschel personified the spiritual imperative of sanctifying God's name in the world.

Heschel marched for civil rights with Dr. King.

Heschel did social Justice like a Reform Jew, critical scholarship like a Conservative Jew, and he prayed with the fiery fervor of an Ultra-Orthodox Chassid.

In a word, Heschel was the first post-denominational Jew.

Today it seems like we have a normative division of labor in which secular people have a steadfast commitment to human rights, whereas the religiously observant have a monopoly on rigorous spirituality.

It's time to break down this dichotomous equation and synthesize the best of both worlds.

It's time to sanctify God's name by combining the political virtues of the enlightenment with the spiritual fervor of traditional religiosity.

It is difficult and exceptional to be both deeply religious and a universal humanist at the same time, but then again, as Spinoza observed in the concluding sentence of his Ethics: "Everything that is worthwhile is as difficult as it is rare."